1

To Glasgow Caledonian University's BA Multimedia Journalism class of 2017. You inspired me to write this and will always be in my heart.

Christina McIntyre worked as a broadcaster and journalist in the eighties, nineties and noughties. She was a news reporter/presenter for Radio Clyde, Grampian TV and STV, working on news and current affairs programmes. She started higher education teaching in the mid-nineties and now works as a lecturer in broadcast journalism at Glasgow Caledonian University. She is a Senior Fellow of the Higher Education Academy.

CHRISTINA MCINTYRE

MIND YOUR LANGUAGE!
Writing with impact for broadcast news

Contents

ACKNOWLEDGMENTS

I am indebted to the many industry professionals who helped with this book, including my editor Stewart Ward, and my reviewers Calum Leslie, Amanda Mezzullo and Dr Helena Bassil-Morozow.

I am particularly grateful to the employers who contributed their wisdom and advice: STV's Suzanne Lord, deputy head of news and editor of news intake at STV; Andy Cairns, executive editor at Sky Sports News; and Bauer City Network's head of news and sport Scotland, Lorraine Herbison, who also advised on current practices.

INTRODUCTION

I've always taken the English language for granted and rarely encountered difficulty writing it. I can't actually remember learning it, as I do French or German, but I clearly did – at school. I certainly recall incorrect spelling, sentence structure, verb formation and punctuation would be circled in red pen and marked down in both homework and exams. This, sadly, does not happen quite so much nowadays. It appears marks are more reflective of students' ideas and analysis rather than their correct use of English language.

As a result, thousands of bright young things do not know how to use apostrophes, how to structure sentences or how to use the correct verb tenses. If you want to be a journalist, you need to be able to write well.

My current role as a lecturer in multimedia journalism at Glasgow Caledonian University has opened my eyes to the key mistakes my domestic students make when writing in their mother tongue. I stress domestic students as our international students, particularly those from other parts of Europe, generally have a much stronger grasp of English. Their vocabulary may not be as extensive, but often their grammar and punctuation skills outshine those of our local girls and boys. Again, this is a reflection on how students from outwith the UK learn English at school. I could dedicate pages to a jolly good rant on this subject but that would be a complete waste of my ink and your time, so let's try to tackle the problem instead.

This book is a basic guide to good writing. Use it to avoid being marked down in your academic work, to please your news editor and to spare your blushes in simple correspondence. The good news is, writing English in a competent fashion is not hard. English is an evolving language. New words being added to dictionaries and our vocabularies are to be welcomed, but standards of grammar are declining, and as more and more mistakes creep in and are seemingly accepted, the future is not rosy. In this book my aim is to help you focus on what absolutely correct rather than just acceptable in today's terms. Learn the rules and your writing will pass any eagle-eyed editor's exacting standards.

I was greatly inspired reading *The Elements of Style* which was originally penned by Professor William Strunk Jr. He self-published what he referred to as his 'little book' in the early 1900s as a textbook for his students. The book was later revised, expanded, and published to the masses by EB White, a former student of the pithy professor. It has been read by millions and its philosophies and advice are as relevant now as they were more than a century ago. It's taken me more than forty years to realise it is not a mortal sin to use a comma immediately before the word 'and' – thank you Professor Strunk.

Following the first few chapters on use of language, the latter part of the book is dedicated to fine-tuning the skills required for broadcast news. There are many existing guides available for would-be print journalists, but fewer aimed at those of you who wish to take to the air-waves. This book is specifically designed to help people who want to be broadcast journalists. Do not expect to be hit with flowery or complicated language. That, to me, is the antithesis of good writing. If you feel the need to doze, or constantly use search engines to understand the words you are reading, I will have failed in my mission. If, however, you've just looked up the word 'antithesis', I refer you to my earlier point regarding grasp of the English language.

GRAMMAR

'One way of describing grammar is as a set of rules which allow us to put words together in certain ways, but not in other ways.' (Leech et al, 2006: 3)

Your goal is to write stylishly but simply. In order to achieve this you must have, above all else, a clear understanding of English grammar. Bad grammar's like bad manners – no-one wants to be accused of it, yet we are all guilty of it from time to time. We are more likely to use good grammar in a formal job application than in an email to a friend, just as we are less likely to put our elbows on the table in a posh restaurant than at home.

'There is no grammatical analogue of the Ten Commandments' (Leech et al, 2006: 14). More's the pity. To communicate effectively you should learn the basics and embrace the principle of grammatical discretion which will frequently get you out of a tight spot. Here are the basics, starting with word classes and their functions.

Nouns

Nouns are things: places, people, objects. The *ball* rolled into the *water*.

Singular v plural

What people seem to have a problem with is determining whether a noun is singular or plural. If a noun is singular it refers to one thing. A plural noun refers to more than one of the same thing. The *ball* – singular. The *balls* – plural.

A *collective noun* is singular. It refers to a group or collection of things or people: a *flock* of seagulls, a *group* of musicians, a *band*, a *team*, an *audience* and so on. If you are writing about an audience it is singular. The number of people in the audience is irrelevant, it is still singular.

The audience *was* enthralled: correct.

The audience *were* enthralled: incorrect.

You may of course have more than one collective noun – you may have as many groups or audiences as you like and then they are of course plural.

Sadly not everyone adheres to this simple rule and all too often collective and proper nouns are treated as being plural. The most obvious example is in football. Teams are generally treated as plural items. 'Rangers *are* at the top of the league'. Rangers is one team but you'd almost never hear 'Rangers *is* at the top of the league' and it's not just because the name ends in the letter s. The same discourtesy is applied to Chelsea. 'Chelsea *have* won the cup.' If you write this sentence on a computer which automatically flags up grammar errors you will find it underlined, denoting an error. It is an error but it's one made all over the airwaves. Right now you have a decision to make. Do you want to write correctly, or do you want to be sloppy and hope no-one picks you up on it?

My advice is learn the right way and then modify your writing to accommodate your organisation's house style.

The BBC news style-guide, which is available online, advocates treating collective nouns, including the government, company, body etc. as singular, with the notable exceptions of football teams and music bands. Football teams, however, when referred to as business concerns should be singular so 'Leicester *are* at the top of the league' but 'Celtic *is* to raise a million pounds through a new share scheme'.

Police can be singular or plural depending on the meaning of the sentence. 'Police *are* searching for a missing man' suggests a number of police officers. Where a police force is mentioned police should be singular. 'The Metropolitan Police *has* cancelled all staff leave ahead of the Olympic Games.'

Sir Ernest Gowers, author of *Plain English,* is on the fence: 'There is no rule; either a singular or a plural verb may be used' (Gowers, 1986: 127). He too advocates consistency rather than correctness. His examples include: 'The government *do* not want to amend' and 'The company *is* doing some work on this' (1886: 173). So his view is you can choose to use the singular or plural form of the verb, but, as BBC Scotland insists, you must be consistent within the same paragraph. Thus 'The firm *has* given an undertaking that in the event of *their* having to restrict production...' (Gowers, 1986: 137) is not acceptable.

A proper noun is the name of something and always begins with a capital letter: Brazil, John, Littlewoods.

Here, as with collective nouns, there can be a problem. When a proper noun, such as Littlewoods, ends with the letter s and therefore sounds plural, should it be treated as plural? The answer is no, but it can sound rather odd.

Here the principle of grammatical discretion comes into play:

When you are faced with the dilemma of

either disobeying a prescriptive 'rule' or awkwardly and conspicuously obeying it, reformulate the sentence so it does not arise. This may be known as the *principle of grammatical discretion*, because it avoids giving offence to your addressees, whether their attitudes to usage are authoritarian or permissive (Leech et al, 2000: 186)

Hurrah – who said you could never please all of the people all of the time?

Try this, as it will often solve the problem of something sounding right but being grammatically wrong, and vice versa. When something feels – and by that I mean sounds wrong to your ear as you read it aloud (for example, 'Morrisons *is* closing ten branches in the North of England') – just reword it. You would feel more comfortable saying Morrisons *is* closing ... but you can't because it's grammatically wrong. Try instead: 'Morrisons' *bosses* are to close ten branches in the North of England.' Adding a second noun – in this case *bosses* – makes the plural/singular conundrum disappear.

'The Celtic squad *is* heading to Madrid' – some nifty footwork there as we negotiate the dreaded football reference without alerting the grammar police.

Think outside the box. When faced with something which sounds wrong but is grammatically correct, and vice versa, rewrite the phrase to satisfy both the ear and the rules of grammar.

The combination of an evolving language and slipping standards often enables writers to get away with grammatical murder. Buck the trend. Aim to be correct rather than corrected. When in doubt, use the principle of grammatical discretion. This means no matter who is marking your essay or overseeing your copy, you will not fall foul. Only deviate from what you know is correct (e.g. using the plural form of a verb when talking about a football team) if you write for an organisation which demands you do so.

Remember to use the singular form of the verb after each, neither, everyone, everybody, someone, no-one and nobody.

None can be used as singular or plural depending on the suggested meaning. When none implicitly suggests more than one thing or person use the plural form of the verb – 'None *are* as pretentious as those who use big words'. If none is meant as *not one* or *no one*, use the singular form of the verb – 'None of us *is* perfect'.

Pronouns

Pronouns are words which are used instead of a noun.

Subjective pronouns

I, you, he, she, it, we, they. The subjective pronoun refers to the subject in the sentence. The ball rolled into the water. It later disappeared. The ball is the subject of both sentences. Having defined the subject as a ball in the first instance we then use it for the second reference.

Objective pronouns

Me, you, him, her, us, you, them. The objective pronoun refers to a person being an object in a sentence who receives the action in the sentence. The objective pronoun is, you might say, second fiddle. This means someone else is the subject. *He* gave *me* a dirty look.The subject is the unspecified *he*, who we must assume has been named earlier. *He* is lead first violin in our orchestra of grammar. The object of the sentence is *me* – second fiddle.

Subjective pronouns become objective in form when preceded by a preposition. A preposition is used to link nouns and pronouns to other words including: under, to, on, over, above, from.

Again, it's probably easiest to square this in your mind by thinking that the subject of the pronoun (he or I) is no longer the star of the show so is secondary, as shown in our examples above. That is repulsive *to me*. *That* becomes the star, the subject, and *me* is relegated to the chorus, the object.

My journalism students take great pleasure in correcting each others' grammar within my earshot. A current favourite is 'Liam and *me*' being corrected to 'Liam and *I*'. Hurrah – they are learning! In this sentence both *Liam* and *I* are subjects. *I* does not become an object, as described earlier; it remains a subject, because no preposition has been used.

Possessive pronouns

My, your, his, her, our, your, their. That's *my* book, *his* pencil and *your* rubber.

Demonstrative pronouns

That, this, these, and those. I don't like *that* skirt but I love *this* top. *These* trousers fit better than *those*.

When referring to ownership – such as that's not mine it's theirs, or, I liked yours better – note there is no apostrophe in yours or theirs. It's an error many people make.

Interrogative pronouns

Who, what, which. Interrogative pronouns form part of a question – *Who* ate all the pies? *What* time is it? *Which* seat is mine?

Reflexive pronouns

Myself, yourself, himself, herself, ourselves, yourselves, themselves. Reflexive pronouns refer back to the subject of the sentence or clause. The subject has already been mentioned. I stood by *myself*. He emailed *himself* a reminder to buy his wife an anniversary card. They nearly wet *themselves* laughing.

Relative pronouns

That, which, who and whom. Relative pronouns indicate a clause or part of a sentence which describes a noun.

She's a woman *who* knows what she wants. Our building, *which* has four floors, is in Knightsbridge. Who refers to the woman, which refers to the building. *Whom* is used instead of *who* when a preposition immediately precedes it. To *whom* am I speaking?

Many people are not sure whether to use *that* or *which* in a sentence. Using *which* suggests the next phrase offers additional information. She wore a long dress, *which* was blue. Note the use of a comma immediately before *which*. The colour of the dress is the extra information. She wore the dress *that* was blue; this suggests we have already heard about a number of dresses including the blue one so the colour being mentioned is seen as information which is essential rather than simply additional to the story. Note there is no comma before *that*.

I suspect many of my students are on commission from the manufacturers of *that* going by the number of times it appears in their copy. Rather than using it correctly as a relative pronoun, they seem to use it as a generic and wholly unnecessary bridge to connect clauses or sentences. *That* is not a conjunction so don't use it in this way. She said *that* it was true. The word is totally superfluous. She said it was true.

Check your copy and see how many times you find a rogue *that*. For fun, replace it with SH*T, then delete all the SH*TS – chances are your copy will then be spot on. NB do ensure you make all necessary deletions before sending it to your news editor/university tutor, prospective employer, or you may well end up in SH*T. I'll admit to borrowing this concept from Mark Twain. His chosen expletive was damn, but then he wrote in the 19th century, perhaps sh*t hadn't been invented.

Prepositions

As mentioned earlier, prepositions are words which are used before nouns, noun phrases or pronouns which connect to another word: to, from, about, of, by.

The woman stood *by* the lake. I took it *from* him. They walked *to* school.

According to legend, the famous UK Prime Minister Sir Winston Churchill was once criticised for ending a sentence with a preposition. The story goes he responded to the pedantic critic saying 'that is gross impertinence up with which I will not put'. The moral of the story, whether it is fact or fiction, is at times it makes perfect sense for you to end a sentence with a preposition, especially if writing in a conversational style. Churchill's witty riposte may have been grammatically correct, but it sounded extremely convoluted. For no good reason, I will treat you to another famous Winnie witticism. Lady Astor to Winston Churchill: 'If I were married to you, I'd put poison in your coffee.' Churchill to Astor: 'If I were married to you I'd drink it.' Ah, they don't make political leaders like that anymore. I can't imagine Theresa May and Jeremy Corbyn exchanging such witty banter, can you? Again this account may not be true, but to quote another proverb: 'Never let the truth stand in the way of a good story, unless you can't think of anything better.' Another little gem from Mark Twain, allegedly.

Conjunctions

Conjunctions are linking words used to connect words, phrases or clauses within a sentence: but, however, although, despite, so, while, until, thus... (The list is pretty long but it does not include *that*). I like children, *but* I couldn't eat a whole one. I often use irony when I write, *and* it is frequently misinterpreted.

Verbs

Verbs are doing words: to run, to hide, to smile. Verbs activate sentences. When we talk of writing in a tense, this is reflected in the form of the verb used. 'He *ran* to the door', '*I'm* on my way', 'the motion *should be* passed' and so on. Verbs and nouns are the cornerstones of good sentences.

Active v Passive

Aim to use active verbs rather than passive verbs. In your quest for dynamic copy the goal is to bring every phrase to life, so active always trumps passive. 'Millions of people speak Spanish' – active. 'Spanish is spoken by millions of people' – passive. Using active verbs is a no-brainer if you want to write in conversational language.

Tenses

In broadcast news, as we are trying to be as up to date as possible, we always try for present or future tenses.

Future tense is pretty straightforward: 'Celtic *will* travel to Madrid for the next leg of the cup.'

The most widely used form of present tense in broadcast news is the *present continuous* tense, which uses the verb *is* + the verb ending *–ing*. 'The foreign secretary is fighting for his political career.' The name of this tense gives us a good clue as to why we use it – we want the news to sound current and thus continuous.

At times we do of course have to use past tense, and in such instances we favour the *present perfect* tense which uses *have/has* + the *past participle* of the main verb.

'A man *has died* in a house fire.' This form of past tense makes the sentence sound slightly less dated than the simple past option of 'A man *died*'. The *present perfect* option also suggests there is more to come, while the *simple past* version, 'A man *died'*, gives the impression there is nothing more to be said.

Look at the top lines I've written below and consider which one you would be more likely to hear on air in a broadcast bulletin. Remember to think about broadcast news copy and not print, which uses different tenses.

The Prime Minister *is heading* to Chequers for the weekend. (present continuous)

The Prime Minister *heads* to Chequers for the weekend. (simple present)

Detectives *launched* a murder hunt in Norwich. (simple past)

Detectives *have launched* a murder hunt in Norwich. (present perfect)

A&E departments in North Ayrshire *fail* to meet waiting time targets. (simple present)

A&E departments in North Ayrshire *are failing* to meet waiting time targets. (present continuous)

Adjectives

Adjectives are words used to describe nouns: A *beautiful* place, *lovely* people. Adjectives add colour to a story but should not be overused. They should serve a purpose and not state the obvious. Don't describe a murder as 'cold-blooded'. All murders, by definition, are cold-blooded.

Adverbs

Adverbs are words used to describe verbs or to qualify an adjective. 'He ran *quickly* to raise the alarm.' That's a silly one – have you ever heard anyone described as running slowly? Perhaps 'He ran frantically' has more merit. According to the author

Stephen King 'The road to hell is paved with adverbs' (2000: 118). In our quest for simple prose, use adverbs, like adjectives, advisedly.

Split infinitive

A split infinitive you might have heard is 'To boldly go' from Star Trek. The adverb *boldly* splits the infinitive *to go*. Split infinitives were trendy in the 14th century, along with syphilis and burning heretics at the stake. Their place is in the past or lost in space. If you are faced with a sentence which sounds better to the ear using a split infinitive, such as 'He strenuously avoided making eye-contact', as opposed to the grammatically correct 'He avoided strenuously making eye-contact', simply reword it to avoid both grammar gaffe and awkwardness. 'He made a strenuous effort not to make eye-contact.' All hail the principle of grammatical discretion.

PUNCTUATION

'Punctuation marks are the traffic signals of language: they tell us to slow down, notice this, take a detour, and stop.' (Truss, 2003: 7)

If you think punctuation's for pedants, think again. The quote above comes from the best-selling book *Eats Shoots & Leaves* by Lynne Truss which rocketed to the top of the charts when it was published in 2003. Truss wrote the book after presenting a couple of programmes on punctuation, on BBC Radio Four.

I'm not suggesting you learn absolutely everything about punctuation as, particularly in broadcasting, you will probably not use it all. Remember – short sentences mean less punctuation. Content yourself with using the absolute essentials, absolutely correctly. Let's start with what is probably the most misused and wrongly omitted punctuation mark of all, the apostrophe.

Apostrophe (')

Little irritates me more than apostrophe errors and I am not alone. More than two decades ago, the novelist Keith Waterhouse had a splendid rant about apostrophes published in his regular Daily Mail column. Founding the Association for the Abolition of the Aberrant Apostrophe (A.A.A.A.), he said the organisation had two simple goals:

> Its first is to round up and confiscate superfluous apostrophes from, for example, fruit and vegetable stalls where potato's, tomatoe's and apple's are openly on sale. Its second is to redistribute as many as possible

of these impounded apostrophes, restoring missing apostrophes where they have been lost, mislaid or deliberately hijacked – as for instance by British Rail, which as part of its refurbishment programme is dismantling the apostrophes from such stations as King's Cross and shunting them off at dead of night to a secret apostrophe siding at Crewe (dailymail.co.uk:2009).

In 2017 the BBC news channel reported on an anonymous apostrophe fixer, who, under cover of darkness, corrected signage in Bristol. This self-proclaimed 'grammar vigilante' (we know it should be 'punctuation vigilante' but it was on the telly so we'll let it go) was so upset by seeing apostrophes in the wrong place or erroneously omitted, he went out at night with ladders and stickers rectifying the errors. In the broadcast, what was Amys Nail's became Amy's Nails, and Cambridge Motor's was changed to Cambridge Motors. None of the business owners whose signs had been corrected noticed, until the change was pointed out. They were slightly bewildered but not in the least embarrassed when their apostrophe catastrophes were aired on national television. If that had been my garage, or, perish the thought, nail bar, I'd have been mortified. Not wishing to climb ladders in the dead of night, I'll opt for prevention rather than cure by telling you in the most straightforward fashion how to use apostrophes.

It's actually not difficult. The first reason to use an apostrophe is to indicate a missing letter or number, usually as a form of contraction: *She's* from *she is*, *he'd* from *he would*, much used in conversational language. Instead of writing 'the winter of 1968', you may write the winter of '68 – again contraction to be more conversational.

An apostrophe is also used when pluralising letters of the alphabet. E.g. 'There are two *a's* in avocado.' 'You'd better mind your *p's* and *q's*.' It also indicates plurals of words – now do not be misled – I don't mean pluralising words i.e. 1 word, 2 words. An example of how you would use plurals of words would be: 'No *if's*, no *but's*'. I doubt you'll have to write such things in your news copy or academic coursework but you never know.

The other big apostrophe function, and this you will use often, is to show ownership: *John's car* – the car belonging to John. *Mary's purse* – the purse belonging to Mary. When using an apostrophe after a formal name do not be spooked if the name, like Charles, ends in s. The same rule applies – it is *Charles's house* – NOT *Charles' house*. There are a couple of irritating exceptions to this rule – ancient names ending in -es and -is and also Jesus. We would refer to *Jesus'* father Joseph – but unless you are a budding historian or theology student I wouldn't worry too much about these irregularities coming up in everyday writing. When showing ownership of a plural noun ending in s such as *masters*, the apostrophe is NOT followed by another s – thus the *masters'* common-room, the *plasterers'* buckets and the *students'* union.

An error I frequently see in my students' submissions is the incorrect use of *its* and *it's*. Its refers to the possessive pronoun. The possessive pronouns are: my, mine, your, yours, his, her, hers, its, our, ours, their and theirs (see page 15). So, just as '*Mary's* handbag' means the handbag belonging to Mary, 'the dog bared *its* teeth' refers to the teeth belonging to the dog. *It's* is a contraction of *it is* – we are back to our conversational language – '*It's* rather windy today'.

The indefinite pronoun – one – does have an apostrophe when possession is indicated – one's parents are looking well. But unless you're terribly posh you probably don't use the indefinite pronoun at all – probably for the best m'lord. *Whose*, the pronoun referring to an associated person or thing ('*whose* round is it?'), is an apostrophe-free zone and should never be confused with *who's* – the contraction of who is.

Perhaps the main apostrophe abomination I encounter is the random adding of an apostrophe when students attempt to pluralise a noun. 'Two *Scot's* were arrested in Spain' – no, two *Scots* were arrested in Spain. To add insult to injury, my students frequently torment me by starting copy with '*Scot's MP's*' – two black marks for them and a lie down in a darkened room for me.

Full stop (.)

The full stop is used at the end of a sentence. It is also used in general writing, including newspaper copy, to denote an abbreviation such as M.P – broadcasters, however, generally omit them, preferring to write MP, MSP etc.

Comma (,)

As a broadcaster I have always used commas to alert

me to make a slight pause in my presentation. If we return to the traffic analogy, the comma is the amber light or give-way sign, whereas the full stop is the red light or stop sign. Both can be opportunities to take a breath. Commas should be used when there is a natural interruption in the flow of the sentence, but you must be consistent.

'She opened the door, looked out, and saw the neighbour's dog urinating on her prize gladioli.' Here commas are required after the words door and out for the sentence to sound natural.

As mentioned in the introduction, whether or not you use commas immediately preceding the word *and* is a matter of choice or house-style. This is known as the Oxford comma. At times you should, as it provides important clarification: 'I love my parents, Justin Bieber and Miley Cyrus.' This sentence suggests the writer's parents are Justin Bieber and Miley Cyrus. Adding a comma before *and* clarifies matters: 'I love my parents, Justin Bieber, and Miley Cyrus.'

Question mark (?)

Surely this is the one punctuation mark which does not require explanation? Use singly. Do not repeat it for 'effect' or you'll look silly. Won't you???

Exclamation mark (!)

If you're in the habit of using exclamation marks, stop it! If you want to write with impact, and I am sure you do, use impactful language. Using exclamation marks is rather like using emojis on text messages – you shouldn't need 'angry face with horns' to convey your rage to the recipient, your choice of words should do the trick. The author F Scott Fitzgerald agrees: 'Cut out all these exclamation points. An exclamation point is like laughing at your own joke' (Cited by Graham, S. & Frank, G., 1958).

A gold star is awarded to all of you now branding me a hypocrite for using an exclamation mark in the title of this book. Thus the moral of the story is: Do as I say, not as I do.

Colon (:)

The colon is most widely used nowadays to denote an explanation of a preceding statement or to show the start of a list. Mae West had one golden rule for handling men: 'Tell the pretty ones they're smart and tell the smart ones they're pretty.' Here the colon introduces the part of the sentence which exemplifies the preceding part.

They introduce long quotes (academic writing) and lists.

'In order to bake a cake you will need several ingredients: flour, eggs, sugar and milk.'

Sorry if I've forgotten an ingredient or two, but my interest in baking is non-existent.

Semi-colon (;)

The semi-colon was historically used to denote a longer pause than a comma (Gowers, 1986: 173) but it is somewhat out of fashion in modern writing, certainly in journalism. In academic writing, it's used to develop a theme; so the part of the sentence after the semi-colon takes the initial point on, and expands on it. Again, not likely to be needed in a newsroom. It's also still used, largely in formal writing, to join two independent clauses within a sentence. 'It's almost midnight; we'll never make the train.' These are two separate statements but they can be linked by the semi-colon to make one sentence. Today, most writers would simply write the two statements as individual short sentences using full stops (King, 2002). 'It's almost midnight. We'll never make the train.' That's what I suggest you do.

Dash (-)

The dash is used as an alternative to the comma and semi-colon. As you'll have gathered by now, I'm a great fan of the dash – it's considered to be a stronger mark of separation than a comma, but less formal than a semi-colon. 'The main reason people use it, however, is that they know you can't use it wrongly – which, for a punctuation mark, is an uncommon virtue' (Truss, 2003: 122). That'll do nicely.

Hyphen (-)

On many keyboards it is the same as the above dash. Like other elements of punctuation, hyphens are less common now than they used to be. As a broadcast journalist, I use them quite often as they can make many words easier to read by avoiding the danger of letter collision. If you write *preeminent* (PRE-EM-IN-ENT) you run the risk of the news reader pronouncing it as (PREEM-IN-ENT). If you use the hyphen *(pre-eminent)* mispronunciation is less likely.

Compound nouns are created when two nouns are joined together, such as *air crew*. Here you have a choice. Option 1 is *aircrew*, option 2 is *air-crew* and option 3 is *air crew*. I generally opt for the

28

second choice as I find it easier to read. Where more than two words are joined together, such as *mother-in-law*, a hyphen is your best bet.

Compound adjectives such as *well-known*, or *up-to-date*, should be hyphenated when the adjective is used *before* the noun.

'He's a *well-known* author.'

But when the adjective is used *after* the noun there is no hyphen.

'His work is *well known*.'

Compound verbs are created when two nouns are added together such as ice-skate. A hyphen is required.

Hyphens can, but do not have to be used, when joining prefixes to other words: *anti-social, pre-holocaust, co-own*. This is a matter of style. It is not mandatory but again I use the hyphen to make the word easier to read. There are times when a hyphen will provide essential clarification. Take the verb *recover* – it is usually used to mean get better or get something back. But it can also mean to put a different cover on something, e.g. a chair. 'I must *re-cover* that chair' and 'I must *recover* that chair' mean two entirely different things. The hyphen is a must if your meaning is upholstery-related. And how about extra-marital sex? Or should that be extra marital sex? Depends who you're sleeping with.

Bearing no relation whatsoever to the last example, hyphens are also required when spelling out numbers, such as sixty-nine.

Ellipsis (...)

We're all guilty of overusing these three little dots...

Ellipsis is rightly used (yes it's singular smarty-pants) to denote words missing from a quoted passage: 'I like this quote about swear words... but I can't be arsed typing the whole thing.' All too often, however, we use the three little dots to end sentences or phrases in a supposedly mysterious or intriguing manner.

'I'd like to say I will, but you never know...'

You're almost asking the reader to fill in the blanks. Sorry, in your quest to write with impact, that's your job.

Parentheses ()

If you like to use parentheses (I prefer to call them round brackets), punctuation, such as commas, should always fall outwith the parentheses as I have just illustrated. I always think of parentheses as an unspoken 'by the way'.

'My daughter went to school yesterday (she hates it you know), and her teacher didn't turn up.'

The information contained within the parentheses is an aside to the main point of the statement. In broadcast copy parentheses are most commonly used to house phonetic spelling of unusual or foreign words: 'The new manager of Paraguay is Chiqui Arce' (CHEE-KEE ARSE). Oh if only they were all like that.

So for the most part you will use: commas, full stops, apostrophes, question marks, hyphens, occasional parentheses, the odd colon, and a sprinkling of semi-colons if you're feeling adventurous – preferably not in the same sentence. You may of course borrow my preferred dash from time to time. Quotations should be encased in quotation marks – there's a surprise. Your house-style will dictate whether these are double or single quote marks. 'The boss shouted: "You're fired!"' Note the quote is treated as a short sentence in its own right within the quotation marks, so it has a capital letter and its own punctuation – here an exclamation mark which must have slipped through the net.

WRITING WITH IMPACT

'Avoid the elaborate, the pretentious, the coy and the cute. Do not be tempted by a twenty-dollar word when there is a ten-center handy, ready and able.' (Strunk & White, 1979: 76)

Fairly recently I was enlightened by a lecturer colleague who told me many academics write to obscure. What a relief. It explains why, on many an occasion, I have lost the will to live a mere handful of words into a book or journal. I don't see the point. Aspiring writers are often advised to write to themselves, but surely the purpose of writing is to enlighten or entertain others? If an author uses ridiculously complicated words for no good reason, isn't he or she just showing off? It's always refreshing to read the works of an esteemed academic like William Strunk whose command of the English language is impressive, yet he does not feel the need to ram it down our throats. The American professor advocates using simple language: 'Rich ornate prose is hard to digest, generally unwholesome and sometimes nauseating... It is always a good idea to reread your writing later and ruthlessly delete the excess' (Strunk & White, 1979:72).

If you are studying journalism at university you will already have discovered there are big differences in the styles of writing required for academic essays as opposed to news pieces. One does not complement the other so you will have to develop two distinct styles to ensure good grades in all your assignments.

As a new lecturer, I was advised to use 'exemplars' in teaching materials. An 'exemplar', to a mere mortal, is an 'example'. When I asked the tutor why he didn't just call it an example he replied, 'That's academia for you'.

Obscurity of language is not just reserved for academia, the civil service has long been tarred with the same brush. In 1948, Sir Ernest Gowers, a distinguished civil servant, was tasked by the Treasury to write a guide to improving official English. His works have been revised and compiled into *The Complete Plain Words*, now in its third edition.

> If any man were to ask me what I would suppose to be a perfect style of language, I would answer, that in which a man speaking to five hundred people, all of common and various capacities, idiots or lunatics excepted, should be understood by them all, and in the same sense which the speaker intended to be understood (Defoe, cited in Gowers *et.al.*, 1986).

In short, write to be understood by everyone.

'Guiding principles that are generally accepted as good practice are to use plain English and avoid technical terms; to address the reader personally (preferably as *you*)' (Gowers *et. al.*, 1986:11).

According to author and journalist George Orwell: 'good prose is like a windowpane' (2014: 85). The author, most famous for *Animal Farm* and *1984,* offers five basic rules for good writing (Orwell, 1945: 230):

1. Never use a metaphor, simile, or other figure of speech which you are used to seeing in print.

33

2. Never use a long word where a short one will do.
3. If it is possible to cut a word out, always cut it out.
4. Never use the passive where you can use the active.
5. Never use a foreign phrase, a scientific word, or a jargon word if you can think of an everyday English equivalent.

Your structure and choice of language will determine whether or not you write with impact. As discussed in punctuation, exclamation marks do not create impactful statements – appropriate words do. Sentence length is also important so use impactful words in short sentences. Your aim is to be short and snappy. Journalists write statements. 'Parliament is in recess.' Statements should always be active. Avoid non-committal, tame, woolly words. Say what you mean and mean what you say.

'She wasn't often punctual.' = 'She was usually late.'

'He didn't consider reading to be a good use of his time.' = 'He thought reading was a waste of time.'

Here both statements have been translated from a negative to a positive making them more direct and impactful.

In terms of specific words, rather than phrases, again be direct.

'Tomorrow's weather is set to be fair.' = 'It'll be sunny tomorrow.'

Be direct, be specific and be definite. 'To be clear is to be efficient; to be obscure is to be inefficient' (Gowers et al., 1986:11).

There is no room for wooliness, especially in broadcasting when time is of the essence. Your words should paint simple pictures for the audience, not leave them wondering what you mean. When you sit down to write you must first work out what you want to say. You have the information, now you must decide how to convey this story to your audience. You must fully understand the story, so get it straight in your head before you start typing. All initial story drafts should be short and to the point. They can always be expanded if feature-length material is required. When you have written your first draft, ask yourself could it be tighter? Is it simple, clear and human? You are a human, writing for other humans, so make sure your writing is human. Put yourself in the position of the audience. What would you want to be told? What would be of interest to you? According to oxforddictionaries.com, the definition of news is: 'Newly received or noteworthy information, especially about recent events.'

The medium to which you are filing will have a bearing on what you say and how you say it, as will the audience. However, regardless of the medium or audience, your language should always be simple and have impact. Do not write more than is required. 'Use no more words than are necessary to do the job. Superfluous words waste your time and official paper, tire your reader and obscure your meaning' (Gowers et al., 1986: 13).

There is no substitute for the right word so make sure you use it. Call a spade a spade, not a digging implement. Omit needless words ruthlessly. As discussed in chapter one many writers have a habit of inserting *that* where it is not needed. Whenever you write a story, read it through and establish if any words should be discarded. Deleting valueless prose will always enhance your story by enabling you to include more relevant information.

Another mistake many aspiring journalists make is to repeat key words. This is sheer laziness. There are very few words in the English language which cannot be substituted by others when required. You should always use what you consider to be the best word for the job first, but to avoid repetition you also need to think outside the box and come up with alternatives. This is not about having an enormous vocabulary. I'm not expecting you to spend your evenings trawling through a thesaurus to learn new words. It's about fully employing the thousands of words you already know.

For example, if you are writing a story about a school being burned down, clearly the school is the subject but you cannot keep referring to it in the same way.

'Detectives are investigating a fire at a *school* in Nottingham.

'*St Andrews Academy* in Brown Street was targeted in the early hours of this morning.

'Fire fighters are still tackling the blaze at *the three-storey building.*'

Rather than use *school* in each sentence I have replaced it with *academy* in line two and *building* in line three.

Take the adjective *sad*. You've used it once as your first choice, now you have to find alternatives.

'The gentleman was sad / unhappy / gloomy /

down / low / blue / despondent / dismal / glum.'

You get the picture? A good way to train your brain to have more words at your fingertips is to do crosswords. Not cryptic crosswords – they'll meddle with your mind – just basic crosswords. I do the Metro cryptic crossword most days (other publications are available), as it appeals to my somewhat warped mind. I also do the quick crossword and have even picked up a few new words. Not big long ones, mind you – words like 'nimbus' (meaning large, grey, rain cloud), which I can't imagine using in a news story but hey, you never know.

So what's the story? You decide. You are in charge of what you write (to varying degrees depending on seniority) and the angle you take on any story will shape how it is received by the audience. You should always write your story with the audience firmly in mind. What may be of interest to you may not be quite so interesting to your mother. Many stories are pretty obvious and you don't have to think too hard about what you're going to include in terms of information – you do however have to think about the order of information and the language you use. Common sense will largely dictate the order of information in any story – and if you apply the adjectives 'simple' and 'human' to your choice of words you won't go far wrong.

Order of information for news writing

Headlines (for print and online) and top lines (for broadcast) are the first thing people see or hear. Their purpose is two-fold:

1. To grab the audience's attention.

2. To encapsulate the story.

'A murder hunt's underway in Derby.' – Radio or TV top line.

'Derby murder probe.' – Print headline.

The audience's interest will be piqued by the words *murder* and *Derby*. This top line/headline does its job. It grabs attention and it encapsulates the story. Anything you write thereafter is supplementary information – detail.

The full broadcast copy reads: 'A murder hunt's underway in Derby. The body of a 22-year-old man was found in a flat in Chase Close in the west of the city, just after eleven o'clock last night. Door to door inquiries are being carried out. The victim's not yet been named.'

The most relevant and up-to-date information should always come first. If you have quotes for print or interview clips for broadcast news, use them at the earliest opportunity. People make stories so let the audience hear from the horse's mouth as soon as possible.

If you are writing a story based on a new study or survey, NEVER start with 'A new survey shows'.

Start with the main finding of the study and then attribute it. 'More than half of primary seven pupils struggle with spelling, according to a new government report.'

Language

If I were to ask you what constitutes style, in writing, you would all come up with different answers. Clarity and simplicity will never go out of style so make these your goals, along with, of course, complete accuracy.

Which reminds me – if you use an online spellchecker in your quest to avoid errors, make sure it is not based on American-English. If so it will want to change *colour* to *color* and *organise* to *organize*. The Americans seem to like Z but not U – handy for *Scrabble* points but not much else. If you can use a UK-English version do, but it won't solve all your problems. It will always query proper names. In this chapter mine suggested changing *Strunk* to *skunk* – I'm sure the eminent professor would not be amused.

All news organisations have guidelines on style, from layout to language. You will be expected to adopt your employer's house-style, which will hopefully be clearly documented. Examples of various media outlets' house-styles are dotted throughout this book.

In higher education this will include a referencing style. My university uses Harvard referencing. I'm not saying it's any better than APA or MLA, and frankly I don't care. All I need to know is that's what I'm expected to use and I do.

If you're aiming for a career in print journalism you'll have worked out by now the difference between a tabloid and broadsheet, I hope. Their styles are markedly different – not only in the type of stories they cover but also the language they use. You'll see witty, or otherwise, puns on the front page of *The Sun*. Not so much in *The Times*. This does not mean one is not better than the other. They are catering for entirely different readerships.

In broadcasting the distinctions are not so obvious. For many years, there was clear blue water between BBC and commercial radio and TV stations in terms of content and delivery. Nowadays there is far less to distinguish them.

So what constitutes good writing? Let's start with what does not.

Jargon

Technical subjects must be translated into everyday English for your audience. On occasion you may have to cover something pretty scientific. You must make it understandable to everyone who might read or hear the story.

We're all guilty of lapsing into jargon at times, especially when speaking to colleagues. The police refer to *males* and *persons*. That's *men* and *people* to us. When they say: 'The perpetrators appear to have gained access to the rear of the premises', they mean: 'The thieves got into the back of the building.' 'In close proximity to', means 'near'.

While researching I was amused to learn uniformed officers refer to detectives as 'superstars' (I detect a note of irony), while CID call uniformed officers 'wooden-tops' (no irony detected here).

Doctors may refer to a *script* rather than a *prescription.* Kim Kardashian and social media fans will know a belfie stick is a bendable stick, designed to enable you to take a picture of your own bottom. It would be fair to assume not many people over the age of 40 know this expression so I do not expect to read it in *The Daily Telegraph* any time soon.

Acronyms

Acronyms are composed of the first letters of a phrase, e.g. UK. They should only be used without explanation if they are widely known. *FA* in sport copy, referring to the *Football Association*, is fine (although in conversation I use it to mean something quite vulgar), but the *A.A.A.A.* is not – even if you did pay attention while reading the punctuation chapter. In broadcast news copy full stops are not required between the letters of acronyms including *eg* and *ie*. When an acronym is pronounced as a word, e.g. *Nasa* (not *UK* or *AA*), only the first letter is capitalised. Abbreviated phrases which do not comprise names, such as *mph* (miles per hour), have neither capitals nor full stops.

Slang

Slang is defined by oxforddictionaries.com as: 'A type of language consisting of words and phrases that are regarded as very informal, are more common in speech than writing, and are typically restricted to a particular context or group of people.'

Slang can also be jargon, with one example being the term *photo-bomb*. Do not confuse conversational language, which we like, with overly informal language or slang, which we do not.

Examples of slang include: *sick* (very good), *pig out* (binge eat), *salty* (angry) and *grass* (marijuana).

There's a fine line between informal and overly informal. What one news outlet may deem appropriate, another will not. A friend of mine was recently told off for using the word 'booze' in her radio news bulletin. The story was about minimum pricing for alcohol. She had already used 'alcohol' in the top line, then 'drink' later on. She used 'booze' as her third choice and it did not go down well. Her argument was she was trying to avoid repetition (I'll drink to that). Her superiors considered 'booze' to be a slang word, thus unsuitable for the target audience profile (ABC1). The offending word was duly removed ahead of the next bulletin. The moral of the story is – your house-style will dictate what's hot and what's not, so stick to it.

It goes without saying expletives are not acceptable, damn it. The regulator Ofcom has helpfully graded profanities in order of offensiveness. Timing is the key. Nine o'clock at night is known as the watershed – the time when TV programmes considered unsuitable for children may be broadcast.

The first list of naughties, 'general swear words and body parts', contains (to my shame) a number of words I have never heard of. Avoid them all, they have no place in broadcast news, but here, for your amusement, are a few examples.

'Milder' words deemed as those generally of little concern include *God*, *arse* and *crap*.

'Medium' words, described as potentially unacceptable pre-watershed but as acceptable post-watershed, include two of my personal favourites, *bollocks* and *pissed off*.

'Strong' words are those deemed generally unacceptable pre-watershed but mostly acceptable post-watershed, and include include *knob* and *twat*.

The 'strongest' words are described as being highly unacceptable pre-watershed but generally acceptable post-watershed. There are just three and you can look them up yourself on the Ofcom website.

Metaphors and similes

A metaphor is a figure of speech in which a word or phrase is applied to an object or action to which it is not literally applicable. *He was drowning in paperwork.* Clearly you cannot drown in anything but liquid. Metaphors should be avoided in news copy.

A simile is a figure of speech involving the comparison of one thing with another thing of a different kind, used to make a description more emphatic or vivid. *'He was a brave as a lion.' 'It was as black as coal'.* By using similes in these two examples you are suggesting your audience needs an explanation of the words *brave* and *black*. They don't, so avoid similes in news copy.

Clichés

Clichés are phrases which, perhaps when first invented, were relevant, but over time have become so hackneyed they are now used in inappropriate contexts or as unnecessarily frilly descriptions. *'No stone was left unturned during the search.'* It simply means they searched thoroughly. Stretching the bounds of reality this might apply to a search of a quarry, but really, did the search team turn over every single stone? Nowadays the cliché is used to describe any type of search – whether stones are present or not. *'When it comes to the crunch'* is another little gem, or horror, depending on your point of view. Again perhaps at some point the expression was used in terms of food-tasting. *'When it comes to the crunch the flavour is fully released.'* I suspect not. It certainly has no relevance when talking about international talks (*crunch talks* being another clanger) where, one can assume, the only crunching taking place occurs when the tea and biscuits are served.

Good practice

Your goal is to write short, simple and clear copy. How do you ensure it has impact? Having denied you exclamation marks, clichés, similes, metaphors, slang, jargon and expletives, you might be worried. Fear not – by choosing the right words, using them in the right places and avoiding repetition, your copy will hit the spot. Make sure you use a dictionary to check the exact meaning of a word if you are unsure and, as with all grey areas, if in doubt leave it out. The dictionary will also help you identify helpful alternatives to guard against the dreaded repetition.

Nouns and verbs are the cornerstones of good prose. Using the most appropriate nouns and verbs will often negate the need for adjectives and adverbs. Avoid pretention at all times. A *prodigious* child is an *intelligent* child. *Intelligent* is a word which is understood by the vast majority of people, *prodigious* is not.

> 'One of the really bad things you can do to your writing is to dress up the vocabulary, looking for long words because you're maybe a little bit ashamed of your short ones. This is like dressing up a household pet in evening clothes. The pet is embarrassed and the person who committed this act of pre-meditated cuteness should be even more embarrassed' (King, 2000: 117).

Adjectives and adverbs can add valuable colour to

44

stories but they should be used in a considered manner and not as a matter of course. Avoid qualifiers: *rather*, *little*, *very*, *pretty*. These, used ahead of adjectives, water down copy rather than augment it. 'The woman was *rather* fat.' Was she fat or not? If so then write 'The woman was fat'.

Compare these example sentences:

1. He *walked* down the street.
2. He *strutted* down the street.

Each has the same number of words, neither contains adjectives nor adverbs, but example two has more impact because the verb used is more descriptive.

1. The report identifies *a number of* problems.
2. The report identifies *a string of* problems.

Again example two is more descriptive. Using *string* instead of *number* is more colourful and, therefore, has more impact. Remember, your job is to paint pictures. Example two infers more problems. A note of caution – make sure your word choices do not leave you open to accusations of editorialising. You would not use the expression '*string* of problems' if only two had been found. If you did, you could be accused of hyping up the story.

Your choice of language must always reflect the house-style of your organisation. Words and phrases acceptable to one organisation may not be to another. Compare the nouns and verbs below, determining which have more impact.

Crash/Smash

'The car *crashed* into the barrier.' Alternatively: 'The car *smashed* into the barrier.' *Smashed* suggests more impact – literally.

Broke/Shattered

'The glass *broke* when it hit the floor.' 'The glass *shattered* when it hit the floor.' *Broke* suggests it may have split into two or three parts while *shattered* suggests it ended up in smithereens.

Try/Strive

'He is *trying* to overcome his fear.' 'He is *striving* to overcome his fear'. *Strive* implicitly suggests more effort than *try*.

Cry/Weep

Used in the context of shedding tears, *weep* portrays a more profound sadness or despair than *cry*.

In sport copy, it's always good to try to convey the circumstances around a result or score:

1. 'Rangers are out of Europe after a 4-nil *loss*.'
2. 'Rangers are out of Europe after a 4-nil *hammering*.'
1. 'Joe Root's side *claimed* the win on the final ball.'
2. 'Joe Root's side *snatched* the win on the final ball.'

Here the nouns *hammering* and *snatched* add more colour.

COMMON MISTAKES

'The difference between the right word and the almost right word is the difference between lightning and a lightning bug.' Mark Twain

There are numerous words in the English language that are regularly misused. Some of them sound similar but have very different meanings. Others have similar meanings but are often written in the wrong context. You'll also find a small number of words which are not real words and which should never be used despite having somehow crept into some unsuspecting speakers' everyday language.

A/An

The indefinite article a or an is used to describe one of something. '*A* man has fallen over.' An is only used if the first letter of the preceding word SOUNDS like a vowel. Whether it IS a vowel or not is irrelevant. Thus: *A* cat, *an* occasion, *an* honour, but *a* hotel.

Affect/Effect

Affect means to influence. 'The weather *affected* play.' *Effect* means to bring about or accomplish. 'The decision did little to *effect* change.'

Allusion/Illusion

Allusion means an indirect reference to something. 'He *alluded* to the possibility of a pay rise.' *Illusion* means an un-real image such as an '*illusion* of grandeur'.

Assume/Presume

There is a subtle difference between these two verbs which both mean to suppose. *Presume* suggests a balance of probability. 'Two hill walkers are *presumed* dead after an avalanche on Ben Nevis.' *Assume* supposes something to be the case without proof or a balance probability. 'I *assumed* he would be on time but he was late.'

Assure/Ensure/Insure

Assure means to promise or say with certainty. 'I *assure* you he's a great poker player.' *Ensure* means to make certain. 'I *ensure* I eat five portions of fruit.' *Insure* means to protect against risk. 'It costs £300 a year to *insure* my car.'

Bail/Bale

The noun *bail* is the temporary release of someone awaiting trial. 'He was released on *bail*.' The verb *bail* means to abandon something. 'I *bailed* after a couple of hours.' It can also be used to mean removing water from a boat. 'I *bailed* out the water with a bucket.' *Bale*, a noun, can mean evil, or a bundle of something, usually hay or cotton. 'The tornado destroyed hundreds of hay *bales*.'

Complement/Compliment

Complement means to complete or enhance. An easy way to remember this different is that *e* is used twice in 'complement' and 'complete'. 'The colour *complemented* her eyes.' *Compliment* means praise, as a noun and a verb. 'He *complimented* her on her outfit.' Note: The adjective *complimentary*, which is often used to mean full of praise ('He was very *complimentary* about the book'), can also be used to mean free of charge. 'You get *complimentary* drinks flying first class.'

48

Council/Counsel

Council is a noun and means an assembly of people serving in an administrative capacity. 'Labour's lost control of *Glasgow City Council*.' 'The *United Nations Security Council* held an emergency session.' 'The *student council* voted to introduce gender-neutral toilets.' *Counsel* can be a noun or a verb meaning advice, someone giving advice, or to advise. 'He kept his counsel.' 'The *Queen's Counsel* approached the bench.' 'He *counselled* him over the bereavement.'

Comprise

Many people often incorrectly add the conjunction 'of' following the verb *to comprise*. 'A zoo *comprises* a number of animals'. The word 'of' is not used next to 'comprise'. *Comprise* means *embrace*, so the zoo *embraces* reptiles, lions etc.

Centred

Things are *centred on* something or somewhere, not *around/round* it. 'The debate *centred on* the rights of EU citizens.' 'The search *centred on* the forest.'

Defuse/Diffuse

Defuse means to make safe e.g. a bomb or a situation. 'His tactful intervention *defused* the situation.' 'Bomb disposal experts have *defused* a forty-pound device found at a subway station in Reading.' *Diffuse* means to cause something to spread. 'The dye slowly *diffused* in the water.'

Discreet/Discrete

These are both adjectives. *Discreet* means careful or tactful. 'He asked *discreet* questions.' *Discrete* means

49

separate. 'Earthquakes were recorded in *discrete* areas of the city.'

Disinterested

This means *impartial*. A football referee should always be *disinterested*. This should not be confused with *uninterested* which means having no interest in something. 'Judges must always be *disinterested*.' 'He seemed *uninterested* in his wife's gossip.'

Elicit/Illicit

Elicit is a verb meaning to draw out or obtain (usually information). *Illicit* is an adjective meaning illegal.

Faze/Phase

Faze means to confuse. 'The last question *fazed* him.' *Phase* means to introduce something in stages. 'The improvements will be *phased* in.'

Fewer/Less

Fewer refers to numbers, whereas *less* refers to quantity. '*Fewer* than ten' is correct, as is '*less* than a ton'. Shame on our supermarkets who advertise the so-called 'express checkout' as suitable for those who have 'ten items or less'.

Fortuitous

Often misused to mean 'lucky'. *Fortuitous* means what happens by chance, so could be *lucky* or indeed *unlucky*.

Gate/Gait

Gate is an entry. 'The field has two *gates*.' *Gait* is a manner of walking. 'Light on his feet, he had the *gait* of a dancer.'

Gotten

Gotten is another fabricated word. An absolute howler sometimes used in error as the past participle of the verb *to get*. 'They have *got off* lightly' is correct. 'They have *gotten off* lightly' should be a hanging offence. Speaking of which...

Hangar/Hanger

Aircraft are stored in *hangars*. *Hangers* are what clothes are put on.

Hoard/Horde

Hoard is a noun and a verb linked to collecting and storing materials, often in secret. Squirrels *hoard* nuts and their collection of nuts could be described as a *hoard* of nuts. *Horde* is a noun and refers to a large group, usually of people but can also apply to other things like insects. 'There were *hordes* of people on the beach.' 'A *horde* of flies invaded the tent.' *Horde* is often used in a slightly negative fashion, such as '*angry hordes*', so be careful.

Irregardless

No such word exists. The word you are seeking is *regardless*, meaning *despite*.

Lead/Led

Lead (pronounced LEDD) as a noun is a type of metal. 'The *lead* on your roof needs replacing.' 'His feet felt like *lead*.' *Lead* (pronounced LEED) as a noun or adjective relates to being ahead or in charge. 'Rangers took the *lead* in the first half.' 'He has the *lead* role in the play.' *Led* means one thing only – it is the past tense of the verb *to lead*. 'He *led* us to safety.'

Licence/License

Licence with a *c* as the second-last letter is the noun – 'driving *licence'*. When the *s* is the second-last letter used it is a verb – 'the pub is *licensed* to sell alcohol'.

Metal/Mettle

Metal is a noun meaning a chemical element such as gold or iron. 'Is steel a stronger *metal* than titanium?' *Mettle* means resilience, determination or an ability to deal with difficulty. 'He really showed his *mettle* in the last set.'

More than/Over

More than should be used when writing about numbers. '*More than* 10.' *Over* should be used when defining mass. '*Over* a ton.' So an easy reminder is if you can 'count' it, use *more than*.

Nauseous/Nauseated

Nauseous means 'sickening to contemplate', so you may well describe animal cruelty as *nauseous*. If you describe yourself as being 'nauseous' you are actually suggesting you yourself are sickening for other people to contemplate. This may indeed be true but as it's not what you really mean you should describe yourself as *nauseated* instead.

Practice/Practise

The easiest way to remember this one is to learn the one with the *c* is a noun and the one with the *s* is a verb. *Practice*, the noun, has two meanings. It can mean facility – 'He owns a successful dental *practice'* – and it can also mean the act of *practising*. 'No wonder he's on the putting green all morning – he needs the *practice.*' *Practise* the verb means repeating or rehearsing something in an attempt to improve. 'I'm *practising* putting four hours a day.'

Principal/Principle

Principal is an adjective or noun meaning *main*, or *chief*: 'The *principal* reason for selecting him was his personality.' 'She is the *principal* of the university.' *Principle* pertains to a standard or belief often related to morals. 'He objected as a matter of *principle.*'

Regretful/Regrettable

Regretful means *showing regret* while *regrettable* means *causing regret*. 'He was *regretful* after the game.' 'The outcome of the game was *regrettable.*'

Rein/Reign

Reins are part of a horse's bridle. Monarchs *reign*.

Sight/Site

Sight is what one sees: 'A *sight* to behold.' *Site* relates to location. 'He works on a building *site.*'

Stationary/Stationery

Stationary means not moving – at a standstill. 'The train was *stationary* for 40 minutes.' *Stationery* is the collective noun for pens, paper etc. 'Do you need any *stationery* supplies?'

Storey/Story

Storey means floor as in the number of floors in a building. 'There are *seventeen storeys* in that tower-block.' *Story* is a tale. 'He read his children a *story* each night.'

That/Which

That is defining and restrictive, *which* is not. 'The car *that* is rusty is in the garage.' This suggests there's more than one car and the rusty one is in the garage. 'The car, *which* is rusty, is in the garage.' This suggests there's only one car and it is in the garage.

The/The

What's the difference? Pronunciation. Normally, we pronounce *the* with a short sound (THUH). 'The sky is blue.' When the definite article comes before a vowel sound, we pronounce it as a longer sound (THEE). '*The* effect was shocking.' The long 'the' (THEE) is also used when we wish to show emphasis, whether the word begins with a consonant or vowel sound. 'It's *the* (THEE) greatest.' Don't overuse the emphatic 'the' or you'll sound like an overexcited football pundit.

Tortuous/Torturous

Tortuous means full of twists and turns or long and complicated thus a winding road could be *tortuous*. *Torturous* means causing pain so a memory might be *torturous*.

Misused words

In addition to acronyms, as discussed in chapter three, there are a number of words and phrases which are much overused in every-day writing and journalism, which should be avoided.

A game of two halves

A much-loved sporting pundit's comment which is utterly superfluous.

At the end of the day

What does this mean? At 5pm? At midnight? News reports are plagued by this awful cliché which 99% of the time has nothing to do with the end of any day. It's used to mean *ultimately*, and as it was voted Britain's most hated cliché, should 'at the end of the day' be deleted from your copy.

Boast

This means *to speak proudly of* but is often misused. 'The arena *boasts* the largest number of seats in the country', should read: 'The arena *has* the largest number of seats in the country.'

Cautiously optimistic

If someone says he is *'cautiously optimistic'* he is simply hedging his bets and telling you nothing. It's a cop-out.

Currently

A largely redundant word. 'We are *currently* reviewing the options.' News is about what's happening now so *currently* is not required.

Foreseeable future

What is that exactly? In ten minutes? A month? Is a crystal ball required? It's just too vague.

Full-scale

'A *full-scale* search has been launched.' Have you ever heard of a 'half-scale search'? No – so ditch *full-scale* – it means nothing.

It's hoped

'*It's hoped* a deal can be reached.' Who's hoping? Tell

us. '*Workers* at Hunterston are *hoping* a deal can be reached.' If you've just written *'It's hoped'* as a way to start the sentence then you are editorialising.

In-depth probe

A *probe* is a blunt surgical instrument used for inserting into parts of the human body to examine them, so *in-depth probe* has particularly unpleasant connotations. Unfortunately *probe* is often used by journalists to mean *investigation* or, as a verb, *to investigate*. You can do better – there are plenty of alternatives. Reserve *probe* as a medical term and when referring to a projecting device used in space.

Jobs blow

This phrase is ghastly tabloid journalese to be avoided at all times. Broadcasters are also terrified they may accidentally transpose the two words on air, so don't risk it.

Last-ditch

This means *final attempt* and has nothing to do with ditches. We hear *'last-ditch bid'* all too often. Just use *final attempt* or *last try*.

Literally

Often used in support of exaggeration and largely redundant. 'He was *literally* shaking with fear.' Here *literally* is superfluous. 'He *was shaking* with fear.'

Meaningful

An unnecessary adjective which adds nothing to a story. 'A *meaningful* discussion took place.' Perhaps this is in contrast to the meaningless discussions which also took place?

Needless/suffice to say

If that's the case you don't need to say it.

Palpable

Means *able to be touched* so 'a *palpable* sense of relief' is overegging the pudding somewhat. *Palpable* is a word you can generally afford to ditch in news copy.

Partially destroyed

Destroyed is an absolute term rather like *pregnant*. Something can be *destroyed*, you can be *pregnant*, but nothing can be *partially destroyed* and no-one can be *partially pregnant*. Something is either *destroyed* or it is not – there are no half-measures. Therefore referring to something as '*completely destroyed*' is a tautology (saying the same thing twice).

Split-second

Be careful using this one. It has its place but as *split-second* literally means within a duration of less than a second it must only be used in this context. A *split-second decision* may be acceptable, but describing a town as being '*washed away* in a *split-second* by floods', would not be.

Today

If it's news it's happening now so you should not generally use '*today*' in your copy. Only if you are differentiating between something which happened at some other point in time should you need to use the word. 'Ministers are finally in agreement over guaranteeing the rights of EU citizens. Following weeks of arguments, *today* a deal was reached.' In an ideal world you would be more specific – e.g. by saying whether it was this morning or afternoon – but using *today* in this context is not a mortal sin.

Thrust

A noun or verb suggesting power, but which also has sexual connotations. Restrict its use to the specific: 'The piston has a *five-inch thrust*.'

Try and

'Try and' Is wrong – the correct phrase is *try to*. 'I'll *try to* remember', not 'I'll *try and* remember'.

Should of

Another phantom combination, all too often used when *should've* is meant. 'He *should've* been there' is a shortened version of 'he *should have* been there'. There is no *'of'*.

Unique

Again a much over-used adjective. *Unique* means *without like or equal* so in layman's terms *a one-of*. Like *destroyed* it is an absolute and there cannot be degrees of uniqueness. Thus 'it really is *quite unique*' is complete nonsense. It is either *unique* or it is not.

Unsung hero

This means someone who makes a substantive but unrecognised contribution. By mentioning them you're in effect 'singing about them' so they are therefore no longer 'unsung'.

Yous

I cannot believe I have to write this imaginary word, but as I hear so many people using it, I feel I must. *Yous* does not exist. It is NOT the plural of *you*. The plural of *you* is *you*.

Tautologies

Finally, a short, brief note on tautologies, which I've written personally (gotcha). A tautology occurs when you say the same thing twice using different words, as I have just crudely demonstrated. 'They arrived *one after the other in succession.*' Omitting the adjective generally fixes the problem. Here are some common phrases where adjectives added to precede a noun create tautologies:

- Advance warning
- Mutual co-operation
- Local resident
- Past history
- Exact replica
- Anti-government rebel forces
- Fellow countryman
- Possible options (an impossible option isn't an option)
- Real chance (if it's not real it's not a chance)

And lastly, remember anything being *launched* is, by definition, *new*, so avoid 'a *new* scheme is being *launched*'.

PRONUNCIATION

'Pupils at Cherry Tree Primary School, in Basildon, are being taught to ditch their Essex accents during weekly lessons from a private tutor. Teachers say they have seen a vast improvement in their pupils' spelling and writing since the lessons were introduced – with some parents even admitting they are now corrected on their pronunciation by their own children.'
(www.telegraph.co.uk)

The standard form of British English pronunciation is based on Received Pronunciation, or RP, which is also known as Oxford English. Linked to upper and middle-class English speakers in southern England, it gradually fell out of fashion after the Second World War and is a rarity on today's airwaves. The Queen uses RP – probably why we also refer to it as the Queen's English. Fashionable or not, correct pronunciation is based on RP and most dictionaries published in the UK, including the Oxford English Dictionary, will give phonetically transcribed RP for all words.

Nowadays, thankfully, regional accents rule the air waves. There is no need to channel Her Royal Highness in your quest to become a broadcaster. In 2008 the director-general of the BBC called for an increase in the number of regional accents heard on the corporation's TV and radio programmes. Well-known news anchors and reporters wearing their regional accents loud and proud include the BBC's Huw Edwards (Glamorgan, Wales) and Dan Johnston (Nottingham, England), along with Sky's Kaye Burley (Lancashire, England) and Eamonn

Holmes (Belfast, Northern Ireland). BBC Breakfast presenter Steph McGovern (from Middlesbrough, England) found herself making the headlines instead of broadcasting them in 2014 when several newspapers reported a viewer had written to her offering £20 to help her pay for 'correction therapy' for her northern accent.

It's cruel and offensive but does the viewer have a point? Just as a spin doctor or publicist should shape the news rather than become the news (just ask Max Clifford), should the news reader not deliver the news without his or her accent becoming a talking point? In Steph McGovern's case there is no way her accent impedes a clear and confident delivery, but there are some broadcasters, who shall remain nameless, who would do well to provide subtitles.

Would-be broadcasters should aspire to Standard English, defined as 'the English language in its most widely accepted form, as written and spoken by educated people in both formal and informal contexts, having universal currency while incorporating regional differences' (dictionary.com). Stop frowning if you're from one of the devolved nations – you're not being ignored – you have your own equivalents, e.g. Standard Scottish English.

Just as our writing should be understood by everyone, so should our speech. Accent and dialect are two different things. Dialect is the words you use and accent is how you pronounce them. As a general rule for newswriting avoid using words and phrases particular to specific regions or social groups. I'd describe the weather as *dreich* to my neighbour but would convert it to *dreary* on air. The accent with

61

which you currently speak is already ingrained if you're old enough to read this book. That's not to say you can't modify it. When I'm broadcasting I don't try to bury my west of Scotland accent and become someone else, but, as in everyday speech, I try to make sure I'm speaking clearly. I dot the i's and cross the t's on air. Lazy speech is bad broadcasting.

If you've grown up among people who mispronounce words as a matter of course, chances are you will do likewise. In a strong Birmingham accent *pie* is pronounced as *poi*, and *pint* becomes *point*. Cockneys are infamous for dropping the letter *h*, so *hospital* becomes *'ospital*, *happen* is *'appen* and so on... *'orrible*.

The popular TV series TOWIE features a group of glamorous young adults whose lives revolve around romantic relationships and clothes. What they lack in diction they perhaps make up for with sparkling white teeth.

In their Essex world, like London's east end, *th* is often pronounced *f* as in *think/fink*. Constant incorrect pronunciation can also lead to incorrect spelling. The show's Peter Pan – Joey Essex – has been known to write *fink* instead of *think* on the mercifully rare occasion he puts pen to paper.

One of the most common errors in speech is the glottal stop – a pet hate of mine. In the UK it usually involves the speaker failing to pronounce a letter, such as *t*, so *butter* becomes *bu'er*. *Glottal* would be *glo'al*. Among those guilty of this are many of my young Scottish journalism students, which is particularly unhelpful considering our country's name has a *'t'* in it. Sadly, *Scotland* becomes

Sco'land, and *Scottish*, which you may notice has two *t's*, is *Sco'ish*. I do tell my students to pronounce at least one of the *t's* in Scottish but my advice falls on deaf ears. Words ending in *-ing* often also fall foul of the glottal stop. *Swimming* becomes *swimmin'*, and to add insult to injury, *berating* becomes *bera'in*, all of which is really annoyin'.

Pronouncing words correctly should not be reserved for special occasions such as being on air. You'll have heard the expression *'telephone voice'*. Don't have different voices, have one – and make the most of it. If you want to be taken seriously in broadcasting make the change now. Pronounce everything correctly in your everyday speech with everyone. You'll never offend. If good diction isn't second nature, when the proverbial hits the fan and nerves kick in, you'll revert to type, which would be a pi'y. This isn't about sounding posh or having marbles in your mouth. Some of the most aristocratic people in the land are guilty of mispronunciation. If you listen to archive broadcasts by members of the royal family speaking 'the Queen's English', you'll note some pronounce the word 'house' as 'hice'. Off with their heads!

We often have to use words from other languages. Usually this will be in the form of proper names, such as place names or people's names. I doubt there is a single professional football team in the UK without at least one international player in its midst. In my early years as a news reader at Radio Clyde, I was frequently nervous reporting the various new signings of Glasgow's two main teams and arch rivals – Celtic and Rangers – who featured heavily in news bulletins and whose players hailed from across the globe. I think it's fair to say there wasn't a Smith or MacDonald among them.

Unlike writing for print or online where all you need to worry about is getting the spelling correct, broadcast copy must be written in such a way as to ensure correct pronunciation. The easiest way to do this is to spell the name phonetically in parentheses. For example: Jose Mourinho (JO-SAY MOW-REEN-YO).

When pronouncing foreign place names, such as Paris, say it in English. The English pronunciation of Paris is (PAR-ISS). The French pronunciation is (PAR-EE). Do not be tempted to use the French version, regardless of whether you speak French, or you will sound like a poser – or should I say... poseur.

Some foreign words, mostly French, are now used widely in English: *en route*, *en masse*, *chic*, *clique*, *depot*, *chauffeur* and many, many more. Avoid them wherever possible and if you absolutely must use one (I suppose *chauffeur* could be unavoidable) make sure you spell it phonetically in parentheses. Just as you would sound pretentious pronouncing Paris as (PAR-EE), you would sound stupid pronouncing clique (CLEEK) as (CLICK). Phonetic spelling in parentheses is the solution to the problem. Do not adopt a French accent when reading them aloud – no rolling of r's (which has nothing to do with twerking by the way). Make the most of your own glorious language; you will find no need to borrow anyone else's.

RADIO

'Writing for radio, where our clients want to be able to cover six or seven stories in two or three minutes, involves extreme discipline and precision. Scripts should be tight summaries of news stories with a focus on a clear top line. Appropriate audio clips to go with cues need to be strong, short and stand-alone, so they make perfect sense in context. Economy of language and clarity are vital because listeners only get one chance to understand a story.' Sky News Radio

Radio, unlike other media, is often a background source of entertainment and information. People listen to it on their way in to work, sometimes they're lucky enough to be able to listen to it at work. For radio news hounds, the challenge is to break though from the background and grab the listeners' undivided attention. Good scripting and engaging audio are essential.

Writing for broadcast is all about durations rather than word counts. If you don't have a computer system which calculates the duration as you write, a rough calculation is three words = one second. An abbreviation, such as *MP*, counts as two words, and numbers should be written in letters. Avoid pound signs and don't shorten *million* to *m*. All this can skew your timing, thus £12m should be written as twelve million pounds.

In radio copy, remember to spell unfamiliar names phonetically in parentheses. Quite apart from warding off a potential spluttering and stammering session by the presenter, it'll help guard against complaints from listeners. You'd be surprised how irate people can become when their names are mispronounced on air.

Unlike print news, which features predominantly past tenses, broadcast news is about the here and now, so present tense is expected. You should not need to write the word *'today'* in broadcast news copy. There is an implicit understanding that everything you are reporting is happening today, unless you make mention of a future date. Yesterday's news is today's chip paper.

The listeners are tuning in to find out what's happening now. What they hear should be different from what was broadcast in the last bulletin. Some listeners will hear only one or two bulletins during their morning and evening commutes. Others will have your station on in the background all day. Ongoing stories should be updated where possible, and rewritten when not, to ensure the news doesn't become stale. It's good practice to write two versions of each story and where a story has audio, edit a piece of audio to accompany each version. Developing stories can run for hours, even days, as long as they are regularly updated with fresh top lines and new audio. A story which ran in the 0700 bulletin, but which is going nowhere, should be dropped after a couple of airings. Your station's style guide will also give you advice on the prominence of audio and how many times the same piece of audio can be used. Usually twice is the maximum. Some news editors believe for a story to be suitable to lead the bulletin it should always have audio. Others may insist on a local story (with or without audio). There's no magic formula.

Returning to the subject of verb tenses, as the news reader is telling the audience what is happening now, all audio clips must also be introduced in the present tense. It would sound silly for a newsreader to say 'Emma Duncan *said* she *was* relieved', immediately followed by a clip of Emma Duncan saying 'I'm so glad it is all over' – clearly speaking in the present tense. Always introduce contributors in the present tense. The main way to omit past tense from broadcast copy is to move the story on. Ask yourself *'what is the right-now angle?'* An easy example is a crime story. You could write 'A man *has been murdered* in Glasgow.' This is accurate but it is past tense. The murder has taken place, it is an event of the past, but do we have to report it in this way? How about 'A murder *hunt's under way* in Glasgow.'? This too is accurate and sounds more up-to-date. We can and should change up the angle to reflect what is happening *now* rather than what has already transpired. That's good broadcast journalism. Naturally there are stories which do not lend themselves to such linguistic jiggery-pokery. Funerals are a classic example. A standard top line would be 'The funeral *has taken* place of the policeman who was murdered in the Westminster terror attack.' Alternatively, 'The policeman who was killed in the Westminster terror attack *has been laid* to rest.' Damned if I can rewrite it in present tense without sounding ridiculous. Another area in which past tense is the only option is court reporting. If you are reporting on what's happened in court that day, it really has to be in past tense. 'The jury *has been sent out.*' 'Sentencing Wright to 12 years the judge Lord

Allenby *said...*'

Here's a rundown of the main ways news is covered in radio.

Copy/Read

When there is no audio to accompany a story your only option is to run the story as basic *copy*, also known as a *read*. Audio is king in the world of radio so copy should always be kept short. Each radio station has its own guidelines on durations but broadly speaking copy should be no longer than 20 seconds.

Cue/Intro

A *cue* or *intro* is copy read by the presenter which precedes audio, which could be a clip, vox pop, voicer or wrap. Cues should be brief. Two short sentences will often suffice, with the last words introducing the person speaking in the audio clip. If the cue pertains to a voicer or wrap, the reporter should be introduced: *'Josephine Christie reports'* or *'Madeleine Dunne has the details'*.

If you are introducing an audio clip of an interviewee you must state the contributor's title and name: '*EU chief negotiator Michel Barnier* warns the Brexit talks will be tough.' Always use title before name. If it's a well-known person such as the Prime Minister you can use her title without her name and then use her name only in a second reference to avoid repetition. The throw-line to the clip can feature either.

Always make sure the throw-line (the last words of the cue which introduce the contributor) do not repeat what the speaker actually says. Thus if Michel

68

Barnier's first words are *'Brexit is going to be tough'* change your throw-line to *'is warning the negotiations won't be straightforward'*. Remember, throw-lines should always be in the present tense.

When faced with a contributor who has a long-winded title or their organisation is not well known, condense the title and summarise the organisation: *'Acting vice-chairman* of the society for the prevention of cruelty to ladybirds Andrew Ward says...' would be changed to *'Insect charity campaigner* Andrew Ward says...'

Example layout

Homeless/Cruikshank 1200 25/8/17

Homelessness in the UK's at its highest level in 10 years. John Smith of the charity Shelter says successive governments have created the problem.

Clip: Homeless/Smith 1

Duration: 12 seconds

Outcue: A disgrace

Total: 21 seconds

Clip/Cut

Sometimes referred to as a *sound-bite*, a *clip* or a *cut* is an interview segment or a short statement made by a contributor. It does not include the interviewers' questions. Depending on your station, the duration of a clip could be anything up to 20 seconds, not usually longer, with commercial stations favouring shorter sound-bites.

Vox pops

Vox pops are short audio clips recorded when members of the public are stopped at random and asked the same question. The answers are joined together to form a snapshot of the voice of the people. Usually a minimum of three contributors is required, with each contributor speaking for just a few seconds. Vox pops are regarded by some as poor man's journalism and many reporters hate doing them. I know only one young reporter who claims to 'love' doing vox pops. As she supported herself through university by being a (rather successful) chugger, this is perhaps not surprising. She finds asking people for interviews even easier than asking them for money.

Regardless of your feelings about vox pops, don't disregard them. They can get you out of a tight spot when it looks as though you might not get any formal interviews. If you're sent to cover a fatal house fire, for example, neighbours may be willing to speak but not wish to be identified. A vox pop (for radio) solves the problem.

A vox pop can also be ideal audio to accompany a light-hearted 'a survey says' type of story where you may welcome humorous responses.

Example layout

Drinking/Vox 1700 31/5/17

Drinking moderately can reduce the risk of contracting Type 2 diabetes. Researchers in Denmark claim a glass of wine, three or four times a week, is better for you than no alcohol at all. Here in Glasgow, the news is going down well.

Vox: Drinking

Duration: 13 seconds

Outcue: off to the pub.

Total: 27 seconds.

Voicer

When a story is important but you have no interview audio to accompany it, reporters can record a *voicer* to justify devoting more time to it. An ongoing court case would be an example. A short cue following the guidelines given in this chapter should end with an introduction to the reporter.

Example layout

Trial/Petrie 1200 24/4/17
The jury in the trial of a man accused of murdering his wife in Nottingham has been hearing how he confessed to the killings. Andrew Petrie reports.

Duration: 25 seconds

Outcue: trial continues.

Total: 34 seconds.

Example voicer script: 'Giving evidence this morning, Detective Sergeant David Wicks told the court the accused, Joe Bloggs, had collapsed on the floor of the family home when police arrived sobbing 'I didn't mean to kill her'. The twenty-six year old claimed he had only meant to frighten his wife Denise when he held a knife to her throat, but when she panicked the blade slipped and fatally injured her. Bloggs denies murder, the trial continues.'

Wrap/Package

A *wrap* or *package* is a combination of a reporter's voicer plus interview clip(s). Atmos sound, which is a recording of audio which is not an interview, may also be included. For example a report about a strike could start with the sound of strikers chanting, which would then be faded down as the first voiceover begins. Reserved for the biggest stories of the day, these are the longest radio packages of all. Durations can range from a tight 40 seconds to a much more considered and detailed piece of more than two minutes. Commercial stations favour shorter wraps often containing single lines of voiceover wrapped around very short interview clips. Note that each wrap should start and end with sections of voiceover (unless you are using atmos), and remember lead-ins to interview clips should always be written in present tense. Your pay-off (final sentence of voiceover) should be forward looking if at all possible, e.g. 'Jones will be sentenced next month'.

Live two-ways

In other words, the *live* voicer or *live* wrap. It will sometimes include cuts to illustrate the story, sometimes not. When there is audio, it's usually the reporter's job to cue into those cuts (you might hear it described as "talking around" the audio). In some cases, the presenter will ask multiple questions and it'll sound more like a conversation. In others, the reporter will simply be cued by the presenter and then deliver their full report (with or without audio), before handing back to the studio. Two-ways are often used where a story is regularly changing and a recorded wrap or voicer is quickly out of date – as it allows reporters to amend their answers to include the very latest. It's a good way of emphasising being live at a big event, and they also work when there's simply not enough time to edit together a wrap or package.

Back announcements

Not often used, but occasionally, following a story with audio, the presenter will read out a short line which ends the story. *Back announcements*, or *back annos* for short, can sound disjointed so should only be used when relevant – such as when a breaking news line drops while the news is on air. For example while an audio clip of the incumbent prime minister is playing, in which she says she is 'considering her position', a helpful colleague may rush into the studio to give you the line 'And we've just heard the Prime Minister has resigned'. A *back anno* can also be used to further promote the story: 'And you can hear the Prime Minister's interview in full in the ten o'clock news.'

Teaser

Some stations favour *teasers* to tempt the audience with what's coming up in the news. Teasers are brief one-liners which can be broadcast at the start of the news bulletin or beforehand.

'Coming up in the news at one – snow storms

73

cause city centre chaos, inflation's up and there's a new face at Ibrox. Join me at the top of the hour.'

These brief statements are designed to hook the audience. Writers will often try to be creative, using techniques such as alliteration.

TELEVISION

'To keep your audience you must tell them a story. The language of television scripting is all about cherishing the pictures and sound and adding to them with the words. That is storytelling. Find the pictures and the sound. Pick the most relevant, interesting or informative. Or just plain riveting, humane, thoughtful or emotional. Then write the words.' (Boyd, 2001: 263)

Many of the principles for writing for radio also apply to TV, especially use of language. Just as radio listeners want simple, conversational language, so do TV viewers. There is one key difference however: while we always strive to use present tense in radio, in TV news, unless it is rolling news, like the BBC News Channel, you will often be filing for an evening news programme. Most regional stations have a flagship programme around 6pm and this is a round-up of the day's news. As such, there will be a variety of stories covered at different times during the day, including some in the morning. More use of the past tense is therefore acceptable.

The most obvious difference between TV and radio is TV uses moving pictures. Television output is a combination of sound and vision, but vision takes precedence.

Pictures

Pictures provide journalists with an even greater ability to story-tell and it is important pictures are used to maximum effect. TV pictures come in a range of sizes, from wide shots, used to show the big picture – excuse the pun – to big close-up shots which would show one very detailed thing, such as an eyeball filling the entire screen – yuck. When the camera is static, the image will also be static, although there may be movement *within* the picture, such as children running about a playground.

Movement shots allow the viewer to see more than one angle of a scene, such as a pan from left to right, or a zoom, which could move in or out. An example of an appropriate zoom would have the camera initially focused on the sign on a building and then zooming out to reveal the whole of the building. Tilts up or down can also be used to good effect.

Choosing pictures

Your opening shot is the first thing the viewer sees. It should be a strong, establishing shot which gives the viewer an immediate window into what is going on. More often than not, a wide shot will be used. So, for example, if you're reporting on a factory fire in Glasgow, the opening shot would be a wide of the building showing the flames bursting out the roof. It would not be a close-up of a fireman.

At such a location you will of course have filmed a number of different sizes of shots showing parts of the building and footage of the surrounding area. These are known as generic views (GVs) or wallpaper. You will also have captured more specific shots, again of various sizes, featuring elements such as a close-up of a sign on a door or a mid-shot of a burnt-out window. Movement shots might include a pan (from one side to another) of a row of fire trucks. You may have filmed a tilt from the ground up to the water being hosed on to the roof. In addition to pictures from a TV camera, 'stills' can also be added to reports. A still, as the name suggests, is a static picture, usually in the form of a photograph or a graphic.

Writing to pictures

Writing to pictures is an essential skill. The first thing you must do is establish what pictures you have. The exercise here is writing to the pictures, not making pictures fit your writing. From time to time you will be in the newsroom and be asked to produce a package from footage already gathered by someone else. These pictures and possible interviews are known as rushes. They'll have been sent in by a stringer or other TV newsroom and you must work with what you get. If time permits, watch the footage before you write anything. TV is picture driven so the shots should drive the script.

If you have been out on the shoot with a camera crew, or indeed self-shooting, you will have been involved in deciding what was shot and what was not. You'll know the best interview clips and the selection of shots available. Always make notes on location. Write brief descriptions of shots and interviews gathered, highlighting especially strong footage. This makes life much easier when it comes to scripting and editing. If you are working as a reporter with a camera operator, sometimes he or she will be off filming GVs while you make calls, set up interviews or sit in a press conference. Communication is the key. Ask your camera operator what footage has been captured so you have an idea before you get to the edit suite. Don't be afraid to ask for a particular shot. If you have a clever play on words in mind, get the camera operator to film a shot or sequence which will serve it. Returning to our fire story, always remember your script is there to illustrate what is being seen, so if you are showing pictures of survivors, write about them as we see these specific shots. Don't talk about several million pounds worth of damage while showing pictures of people. If you are talking about what the fire crews are doing, show them in action. This may seem pretty obvious but you would be surprised by how many people don't execute this well.

Pictures tell a story in their own right. Your script or narration is there to complement what appears on the screen, perhaps to explain it in more depth, but it is NOT there to state the obvious.

For example, imagine you are looking at a TV report of the Prime Minister disembarking from a plane ahead of a meeting with German Chancellor Angela Merkel. You would not expect to say: 'Theresa May walks off the plane at Frankfurt airport.' What does that add to the story? Going back to the picture itself, it would show at least part of the plane, the steps leading down to the runway, and Theresa May (from head to foot). You might write: 'Anticipating a bumpy ride, Theresa May puts her best foot forward as she prepares for Brexit talks with Angela Merkel.' Here you are using the pictures to create a slight play on words with 'best foot forward' while explaining to the viewer what the story is about.

There is more scope to write creatively in television news because the pictures are telling a large chunk of the story for you. The script is there to enhance what the viewer sees.

Using sound

As mentioned earlier, audio shouldn't be forgotten on TV. Even though it's not the star of the show, as it is in radio, it still has an important role.

Natural sound (with pictures) can be used very effectively as up-sound, which means you do not need voiceover or interview clips throughout the full piece. Allowing for around 10 per cent of the piece to be pictures with up-sound makes a more creative piece. Examples include chants from a crowd on a protest march, audience members laughing at a speech, and part of a song being sung during a concert. Up-sound can be used at any point in a package to good creative effect.

All interviews will of course have sound, including vox pops. Unlike radio, which can offer an element of anonymity, TV interviewees are immediately identifiable unless a particular filming or editing technique has been used to guarantee anonymity. As such, vox pops, in particular, can be much trickier to obtain for TV than radio. The guidelines are the same, requiring at least three contributors, but for TV you must ensure their backdrops are different and alternate the direction in which they are facing – i.e. left, right, left or vice-versa. As in radio, many reporters detest this task. Sometimes you'll get lucky – people will be attracted to the camera, curious about what you're doing, or they'll recognise you 'off the telly'. Often they'll be drunks or weirdos but you take what you can get. My most memorable vox pop took place in Glasgow in 2003 when I was a reporter for STV. At the morning meeting I was unexpectedly assigned the 'and finally' story of the day, which would usually have seen me grinding my teeth down to my gums. On this occasion, I viewed it as a challenge. The then Scottish Socialist Party MSP Rosie Kane was calling for the expression 'ned' to be banned from use in parliament, claiming it was a slur on all young people. The irony of this will not be lost on those of you who know your history of Scottish politics. This was the story I was assigned. As we know, it's people who make stories (and I don't mean politicians), so obviously my big challenge was to find and interview some 'neds'. Just think about this for a moment. How do you find neds? There is no Ned Society. Who is a ned – or more to the point, who would actually admit to being a ned? You can't just interview random youths and then portray them on TV as neds. Nor can you go up to someone in the street and ask 'Are you a ned?' unless you want a Glasgow kiss (head butt). Out on Sauchiehall Street, inspiration struck. Four youths wearing hoodies were hanging about together near one of the seats. I approached them, told them the story I was covering and suggested, for a laugh, they might like to *pretend* to be neds and be on the 6 o'clock news that night. Amazingly they agreed. They hammed it up no end. The hoodie hoods went up, they swaggered down the street and did short interviews in Glaswegian accents so pronounced even Rab C Nesbitt might have struggled to 'ken whit they wur sayin'. The pièce de resistance was my piece to camera in front of the bench on which they were all sitting, muttering darkly about 'whit a pure brasser it wus tae be called neds'. It was all going terribly well until, as I uttered my very last word, one got rather carried away with his own performance and said loudly: 'Aye pile of pish!' I corpsed, they then too fell about laughing. I won't tell you how many further takes I needed.

Pieces to camera (PTC)

A *piece to camera (PTC)* is a short segment in which the reporter speaks directly to camera. So, why do we use pieces to camera?

Firstly, we use them to fill gaps in a story where we have a shortage of pictures. For example, in a court story we do not have footage of the judge sentencing the accused. We just have his/her words. Often here a reporter will do a PTC outside the court starting with words such as: 'Sentencing Joe Bloggs to two years in jail, Sheriff Joseph Brown described him as a twisted individual who preyed on vulnerable elderly women.' A PTC can also form an effective bridge between two narratives, usually involving a marked change in location, where using pictures alone either fails to adequately convey the change, or is jarring.

The second main use for a piece to camera is as a branding tool for the broadcaster, to show its presence at an event or location. *Emma Storr reporting from the European Games at Baku for GTV*, proves GTV was there!

You'll have noticed there are some high-profile TV journalists who frequently appear in vision several times in their own reports. The BBC's political editor Laura Kuenssberg is one of them. Perhaps they have a different brief. It certainly appears that way.

Where does a PTC fit in a report? Most often, a piece to camera is used as a pay-off, thus at the very end of a report. This is its most likely position in a recorded piece. Some stories will lend themselves to having a PTC mid-point. Where they are least likely to be used is at the start of a piece. You, the reporter, are NOT the subject of the story so we really should NOT see you first.

The most widely used shot for a PTC is the mid-shot whereby the reporter's head and shoulders are in shot down to just above the chest. This is your typical straight PTC such as outside court. The size of shot will determine how much you can gesticulate. If it's tight, stay still. Using your hands as you speak will only work if we can see them. Otherwise the viewer will be treated to one or two shoulders waggling about, which will look weird. Wider/longer shots will enable you to be more expressive in terms of body language but don't overdo it. Sometimes you will have the chance to be more imaginative. You might do a walking piece to camera where you start in one location and move to another, demonstrating a connection. You might use a prop, an umbrella blowing inside out to highlight gale force winds. In such instances you will most likely use a much wider/longer shot so you are seen from head to toe. A piece to camera in flood water with waders on might start as a mid-shot and pull out to reveal you up to your thighs in water. This would be much more effective than just seeing your head and shoulders. The background must always be relevant. Outside the court is an obvious example. If you are doing a PTC related to a protest march, if you can, walk with the marchers as you do the PTC. As with all filming, check there is nothing inappropriate going on in the background. If there are people, you will always run the risk of someone making an unfortunate gesture behind your back. It's happened to us all. If this is the sort of scenario you are in, do more than one take for backup. In an ideal world, find a spot where the march can be in the background but not right next to you, such as from a bridge with the others below. Sound can also cause problems. Make sure you are not drowned out by busy traffic or shouting protesters. Move to a better spot.

One of the most challenging (and exhilarating) pieces to camera I did was in a helicopter – well, *half* in a helicopter. The story was the end of the search and rescue service at HMS Gannet in Prestwick. The cameraman travelled in one chopper and I flew in the other. Thoroughly rattled following the safety brief, for once I was not worried about my hairdo, but was scared witless of drowning. We'd been told how to 'elbow out the window' in the event of plunging into the North Sea and I'm afraid I didn't embrace the prospect. After we filmed RAF personnel staging a mock rescue, the pilots flew the two helicopters side by side so the cameraman could film me, with my legs dangling out the door, radiant in an oversized orange flying-suit, doing a piece to camera. Visually it was great but the sound was pretty terrible. Rather a lot of wind and engine noise, unsurprisingly.

Remember, the PTC is not designed simply for you to get your face on the telly. It should be used to fill a gap in pictures (see earlier court story example) or it should add something in terms of creativity. At

83

worst it is demanded as part of your employer's house-style. Don't be afraid to try out different ideas and if you're lucky enough to be working with a camera operator rather than self-shooting, ask his/her opinion on what works best. Make sure you have the most suitable microphone for the job. In an ideal world, we don't want to see the microphone in shot, but if there is no way round it, such as in a full length shot, then a clip mic will be the most discreet.

Rehearse your script, keep it short, snappy and in good broadcast style. Maintain strong eye-contact with the camera lens. I'm sure I don't need to say you should not be looking at notes – if you are unable to remember 15 seconds of script then you are in the wrong job. Remember to convey emphasis and emotion through your body language and facial expressions (within reason and taking shot size into account), as well as your voice.

TV story formats

Read/News in brief (NIB)

This is a story which has neither accompanying pictures nor audio. The presenter simply reads the story to camera. In terms of duration it should be as short as possible, no more than 20 seconds.

Underlay/Overlay/OOV(out of vision)/Float

The first part is read by the presenter to camera, and then pictures are played in while he/she keeps reading. Usually no longer than 30 seconds in total.

Cue/Intro + clip/SOT (sound on tape) or Underlay/Overlay/OOV + clip/SOT

The presenter reads an introduction of a couple of

sentences which may or may not be followed by pictures played over the voice (OOV) and leads into an interview clip. Intros should be brief, 10-15 seconds (without OOV), and the clip can range from as few as 10 seconds to 30 seconds (for commercial TV news shorter is better). The name of the contributor who is speaking in the interview clip will appear on screen at the start of the clip by way of a caption. Line one of the caption is the person's name. Line two is their title or the name of the organisation they represent. As TV has captions there is no need for the interviewee to be introduced as part of the cue script – unlike radio.

E.g. Professor John Cook
    Glasgow Caledonian University

Cue + Voicer

Just as in radio this is a report by a correspondent or reporter containing no interview clips or vox pops. In terms of sound, it is just the journalist's voice, but of course in TV the voiceover is covered by pictures. The cue should be two short sentences with the last words serving as an introduction to the reporter, e.g. 'Jack Stanners has the story'.

Cue + Package

Like a radio wrap, the package includes voiceovers, interview clips and in some cases, a piece to camera.

Those are the main formats for news output produced in-house. Now, to what I would consider to be the pinnacle of TV reporting – going live.

LIVE REPORTING

'One of the greatest strengths of television is its ability to show events as they happen. In the "you are there" tradition, viewers are able to witness events vicariously in real time.' (Casella, 2013:362)

In my reporting days at STV I was never happier than when I was reporting live. The adrenalin buzz is impossible to fully describe. It's way better than sex. Those few seconds when the gallery director counts you down: 'five, four, three, two, one and CUE'. I'm getting goosebumps just writing about it.

Satellite facilities, which are expensive, are usually reserved for the most important stories, although logistical considerations such as geography or even a complete lack of pictures can also apply.

There are three main types of live reporting. The first is a simple interaction, with the news presenter handing over from the studio to the reporter on location. This is known as a live two-way. An example introduction would be: 'Hundreds of people have been evacuated from their homes in Spain as forest fires threaten to spread into towns. Our reporter Joe Gardner is on the outskirts of Malaga – Joe what can you tell us?'

At this point the reporter launches into the report, speaking directly to camera. He or she may, or may not, answer subsequent questions from the presenter. If so, the questions have been written by the reporter so do not come as a shock.

I say that, but on occasion a 'helpful' producer might throw a spanner in the works and change a question, without informing the reporter on location.

If you ever hear a reporter or correspondent say to the presenter 'That's a good/interesting question' mid-way through a live report, the rough translation is: 'You b*stard – that's not what you were supposed to ask me.' It can be useful to incorporate at least one question from the studio to break up a live, especially if it's a long one. White observes:

> 'Some reporters have an amazing ability to memorise scripts. For most reporters, however, memorising one minute of copy presents a problem. Most stations and networks have no problem with reporters glancing down at their scripts during live reports, particularly a breaking story. It's less acceptable, however, in a routine live report' (2005:254).

Adding a question from the presenter enables the reporter to divide the report into two or three sections, which makes it easier to memorise and deliver. As the question is anticipated, it can offer a couple of seconds' valuable breathing space. If, as described earlier, the question is not as anticipated, it can prompt a brown trousers moment.

The two-way live can also be done in-house in the form of a newsroom link. This often happens when a news story breaks just before a bulletin or programme. There's no time to scramble a satellite truck and head to location so you'll do a live report from somewhere in the building, often the newsroom. Here you don't need to worry about the environment – no-one's going to walk behind you and do a V sign. There is a different pressure though, as you have colleagues only a few feet away, staying silent, listening to your every word. You may find this more nerve-wracking than being on location.

The second type of live broadcast follows a similar format to the aforementioned but includes a live interview between the reporter and a contributor on location. The BBC calls this a *donut*. Following the introduction from the studio the reporter speaks for a few seconds, straight to camera, and then introduces an interviewee. The camera angle will then change to focus on the interviewee or a wider shot of both the interviewee and the reporter. It is up to the reporter, of course, to control the duration of the interview. This can be tricky. A nervous interviewee may clam up, while an experienced interviewee, such as a politician, may milk the air-time for all it's worth. Not wishing to interrupt the flow, the reporter, who is often off camera or at least not face-on, will use body language as part of the control technique. Nodding encourages the interviewee to continue in the same vein. Doing the 'slitting throat' gesture suggests 'shut up pronto'. At the end of the interview the reporter wraps up the piece by turning back to camera, speaking for a few seconds and handing back to the studio.

The third and most widely used form of live reporting for evening news round-up style shows involves the presenter handing to the reporter who speaks to camera for a short period of time, usually 10 to 15 seconds, then introduces a recorded package, before coming back on camera and handing back to the studio. This is the easiest one as you have a little downtime while the recorded report is playing. Don't get too comfortable – you never know when there might be a technical fault and you appear back on camera unexpectedly. How embarrassing would it be if you were picking your nose?

With all live reports timing is crucial. You will have been given a duration to fill and you will have a director speaking in your earpiece. Rehearsing will help, but little can prepare you for the impromptu change of plan, which happens occasionally. There you are, coming to the end of your well-rehearsed script, when the director suddenly asks you to 'pad for 20 seconds' as the next item has failed to make its hit-time. Deep joy. Try not to let this unwelcome interruption throw you off your stride. You've said pretty much all you have to say – what to do? Don't, whatever you do, slow right down and hope to stretch out your last few sentences. In an ideal world you'll have a little snippet of information you've not already used which can seamlessly be added on at the end. As we don't actually live in an ideal world, chances are you won't, so, as your temperature rises and your palms start sweating, you may have to settle for a simple *recap* of the main points. It's not ideal but your number one priority is to make sure you fill the extra time you've been asked to. I remember this happening to me on several occasions and every time it did I always ended my suddenly extended piece with 'back to you', which roughly translates as 'I've done my bit pal – now it's over to you'.

Many reporters get a huge buzz out of live reporting but others hate it. It can be highly nerve-wracking. If you make sure your script is simple and concise, that's at least one thing you won't have to worry about. You're live, so you only get one shot at it. How do you remember what you want to say? Many reporters choose to memorise key points of information and ad-lib round them. Others prefer to memorise the whole script word for word, especially when covering stories which have legal content, such as criminal trials.

Try out both approaches and see what works best for you. Stand tall, speak confidently, maintain good eye-contact with the camera lens and enjoy the ride.

INTERVIEWING

'Interviews are the mainstay of story-telling in broadcast journalism – first-hand eye-witness accounts from people at the heart of the story'. (Hudson and Rowlands, 2008:89)

Who?

People make news and as a journalist it is your job to find the right people and interview them. Every day, organisations and campaign groups send news releases to the mass media hoping their 'stories' will be picked up. This fodder can be useful to fill bulletins and programmes but only if it is made meaningful. 'New surveys' are a good example of this. Let's say the charity Shelter issues a news release detailing new homelessness figures. Who do you want to interview? I hope your automatic reaction is NOT to say a Shelter spokesperson or a politician. Your main goal is to find a case study, in this instance someone who is homeless, who can talk about what it's really like. Yes, you may also do an interview with the charity and you may also seek political reaction, but the number one aim is to find the case study. This person will bring the story to life and make it worthwhile. Discerning news editors may even refuse to run a story if a case study cannot be found so remember this and act accordingly. As a journalist one of your most prized possessions is your contacts book. Fill it with people who can talk first-hand about issues.

When it comes to using experts, beware the over-exposed. In news programmes you'll see and hear the same old interviewees time and time again... the political pundit, the scientist... it becomes very boring. Try not to use the same interviewees as everyone else. Find your own, new experts. Universities, for example, have lists of academics who should be able to provide a sound-bite or two. Find out who they are.

How?

Good interviewers are great listeners – you have two ears and one mouth for a reason. Your job as an interviewer is to get answers. For most journalists, the majority of interviews are non-combative fact-finding missions. Sorry to disappoint you but highly-publicised gladiatorial sparring contests, when you hear as much from the interviewer as the interviewee, generally only take place during political interviews.

When you embark on a story you may have little time for research. It's not unusual to turn up in the newsroom and be sent straight to a story, news release in hand. 'Don't take off your coat' was a favourite expression of one of the STV news editors when I worked there. All too often reporters are dispatched, news release in hand, the minute they're in the door.

You may well have to mug up on your story as you make your way to the location. The internet and social media have made life considerably easier for news hounds, with information on a multitude of topics just a click away. Nonetheless, journalists are expected to be able to get a handle on any topic under the sun – in a matter of minutes. One day you could be reporting on a nuclear waste story, the next it's a rail strike. You have to write convincingly about everything, so in knowledge terms, many journalists are jacks of all trades and masters of none.

Preparation for an interview should be as thorough as time allows, but not over the top. Don't write down 10 questions you want to ask – write three or four and be prepared to amend your line of questioning depending on what the interviewee says. That means listening. Many young journalists make the mistake of focusing so much on their questions they pay little or no attention to the answers. They believe if they ask good questions (prepared in advance) they will automatically get good answers. Good questions are important, but the ability to listen to answers and react accordingly is even more important. Most interviews will be recorded so this gives both parties the opportunity to correct mistakes. If, for example, an interviewee caught up in the drama of an event or the excitement of being interviewed on TV drops an inadvertent 'F-bomb', the reporter will have to stop the interview and ask the question again.

What is a good question?

The best questions are open questions, meaning a question to which a respondent cannot simply answer yes or no. Open questions usually start with *who, where, what, why, when* – known as the 5 w's. There is a sixth – *how* – and don't forget it, because it can be extremely useful.

Breaking news stories offer little opportunity to prepare in advance. You could be sent to a fire which has broken out in a city tower block. What's the plan?

You should be aiming to interview a fire chief and some local residents, as soon as possible. Apply the theory of first come first served. Obviously if a news conference has been scheduled that will affect your plan but assuming there is not, as soon as you are on site, start asking questions.

'What happened?' is often a good start. It's a non-confrontational opening gambit which will not unnerve your interviewee and will get you some much-needed information.

At this stage you know nothing other than there is a fire in a block of flats. You want to know when it started, how it started (you probably won't get an answer to that question at this stage), any casualties or fatalities, who was involved, what's the state of play now. An opening question of 'what happened?' will give you some background and enable you to pose further questions when you get the answer.

Professional interviewees

If you are interviewing a formal figure, such as a fire chief, expect factual answers. You will learn when the fire broke out, when the appliances arrived at the scene, how many fire engines and personnel are in attendance. There may be detail on rescues and evacuations, possibly casualties or fatalities. You will always be told an investigation is under way into the cause of the blaze.

You will learn the facts, but this particular interviewee is unlikely to give you colour. Most people in positions of responsibility who are likely to be put up for interview by their organisation have had media training. Media-trained professionals have been schooled in the art of getting their key message or messages across. If they ask what your first question will be before you start the interview it's a dead give-away – they've had media training.

On the plus side, the best have honed their skills over a number of years, making them masters of the sound-bite, which is particularly helpful for radio and TV. On the downside, they may not directly answer your questions, sticking instead to the party line. A particular favourite response to a question they don't intend to answer is: 'I can't comment on that but what I can say is...' (and back we go to the key message). If they say 'I'm glad you asked me that question', they actually mean 'I thought I made it clear before the interview started I wouldn't be talking about that – you git'.

If you're likely to fire a claim or accusation at someone, make sure you can back it up. You'll look really stupid if the tables are turned on you and you're left mouthing like a goldfish.

Interviewer: 'Critics are saying this plan's flawed.'
Interviewee: 'Really? Name three.'

Members of the public

Colour will come from case studies and other informal interviewees – members of the public. 'Interviews are the mainstay of story-telling in broadcast journalism – first-hand eye-witness accounts from people at the heart of the story' (Hudson and Rowlands, 2008: 89).

Unlike an interview with the fire chief, you cannot predict what members of the public will say. Asking an eye-witness *what happened?* could provoke a multitude of different answers. He or she may start talking about hearing a bang, seeing flames shoot up the building, or people screaming – you just don't know. Have your ears on elastic and be ready to maximise your opportunity. Members of the public, thrust unexpectedly into the media spotlight, need to be guided and encouraged through the interview process. You guide with questions and you encourage through body language. If someone is telling a tale, encourage them to 'go on' by nodding. You may lean slightly towards them but don't crowd them. Keep good eye-contact. Eye-contact is important in all interviews – it's good manners above all else. It is particularly important when dealing with members of the public who are looking to you (literally) for guidance and, to a certain extent, approval. If you're scanning your notes and not looking as though you're paying attention to what's being said, they may lose confidence and dry up. Do NOT, however, interject vocally with 'OK', 'uh-huh' etc. It can be disconcerting to the interviewee who may grind to a halt. It can also make editing a nightmare.

Listen silently but intently to what's being said and be ready to ask supplementary questions.

Your prime target is someone who has escaped from the blaze or, if there are fatalities, someone who lost a family member. This may sound callous, but it's people who make stories and the more involved they are, the greater the impact will be.

There's a huge difference between a 'miraculous escape' story and a 'fire tragedy'. Someone who has escaped unharmed from a burning building may be quite happy to talk to you, to relive their lucky escape. Someone whose elderly mother has perished, because she couldn't get down the stairs in time, is a completely different proposition. Will such a person give you an interview?

> 'The challenges inherent in breaking news multiply exponentially when the situation requires that you must ask a victim, a witness or a family member or friend suffering through shock and horror for an interview. In fact, some would argue that no one should intrude on the mother who has just learned that her child has been murdered' (Bucqueroux & Carter, 1999: 19).

You can argue about the morality of intruding on grief if you wish, but do it *after* you've tried to get the interview. Your news editor will expect you to get the best of what's available. If you don't even *ask* for an interview and a competitor gets one, woe betides you. Here are some of the guidelines the BBC provides for its journalists:

We must balance the public interest in the full and accurate reporting of stories involving human suffering and distress with an individual's privacy and respect for their human dignity. We must justify intrusions into an individual's private life without consent by demonstrating that the intrusion is outweighed by the public interest. We should normally request interviews with people who are injured or grieving following an accident or disaster by approaching them through friends, relatives or advisers.

We should not:

- *Put them under pressure to provide*

interviews
- *Harass them with repeated phone calls, emails, text messages or knocks at the door*
- *Stay on their property if asked to leave*
- *Normally follow them if they move on*

The death knock

If you are faced with the dreaded *death knock*, introduce yourself and your organisation, be polite and respectful and simply say: 'Could I ask you a few questions please?' The worst that can happen is a refusal. If so, be gracious and move on to someone else. Don't argue the toss. No news editor will admit to encouraging reporters to harass people. The good news is you'll be surprised how many people actually agree to be interviewed in the most trying circumstances.

If you get the go-ahead, strike while the iron's hot. Carry out the interview there and then. It goes without saying you are in the right place at the right time so don't even consider arranging the interview for a later time unless that's what's being offered.

If interviewees are experiencing grief or trauma you must be careful. Your mission is to get the story from the horse's mouth, but you must do everything you can to put them at ease. Quite apart from being nervous about speaking to a journalist, this person may be in a state of shock. Do not add to their problems. Be polite, friendly and above all respectful. Ask an easy opening question, one designed to get information rather than an overly emotional response. You do not want your interviewee to burst into tears at the first question or the interview may well be aborted. Again *'what happened?'* is usually as good a start as any.

If the person has lost a loved one do not ask *'how do you feel?'* – it's an insensitive and frankly ridiculous question. The person will tell you how they feel as they answer other, less obvious questions. Let them talk – don't put a time limit on the interview (unless of course it is live on air which is unlikely in such circumstances). Remember not to interject vocally but encourage through positive body language.

If your interviewee becomes emotional, show an element of sensitivity. Pause the interview to allow them to compose themselves. In TV you may be expected to capture them crying on film. Don't be so naïve as to think this won't be aired. It will. I've been asked on countless occasions 'Did you get tears?' Yes, it's callous, and I hated doing it, but for many journalists it's part of the brief. As soon as the camera has recorded a couple of seconds of tears, switch it off and make sure your interviewee knows it's switched off. Assuming it is recounting the story which has caused the tears and not inappropriate questioning, you will be able to restart the interview when your contributor has collected their thoughts. Only recommence filming when the interviewee is calm and comfortable, or as comfortable as can be expected under the circumstances. As in everyday life, being polite and respectful goes a long way.

After the interview thank the interviewee and tell them when the interview will be broadcast or published. Provide your contact details and ask for theirs along with permission to make contact at a later stage.

Some theories suggest journalists provide a form of therapy when interviewing trauma victims. That might make you feel better about what you do, but I think it's fairer to say we do these interviews because they're an essential part of the role, for our own glory, and to beat our rivals. If, in some way, our interviewees benefit, it is no more than a fortunate coincidence.

WHAT EMPLOYERS WANT

A huge thank you to the following broadcast journalism employers, who took the time to contribute to this chapter, providing valuable insight into what industry bosses really look for in new recruits: Andy Cairns (executive editor, Sky Sports News), Lorraine Herbison (head of news and sport Scotland, Bauer City Network), and Suzanne Lord (deputy head of news and editor of news intake at STV).

Which academic qualifications do applicants require for an entry level position within your news organisation?

Suzanne Lord: Usually we say a degree or equivalent practical experience.

Lorraine Herbison: It depends really. You will always be noticed if you have some form of specific journalism qualification whether it be a degree or postgraduate qualification. This is how most staff get their first job and is most preferable. I have one member of staff who just has a degree (not in journalism) and no official journalism qualifications. Her attitude and work ethic landed her the job. We gave her on-the-job training as well as sending her on a Bauer Academy journalism course to improve her skills. We would consider anyone who has been to study our journalism courses at the Bauer Academy.

Andy Cairns: The pace of our newsroom means we are not an ideal entry-level employer – candidates benefit from having experience at slower-paced newsrooms before coming here. However, we do offer entry level at apprentice level (one per year on Sky Sports News). We also offer a graduate trainee programme (one place per year on Sky Sports News) where we ask for a degree (it doesn't have to be in journalism), qualifications from an accredited journalism course (can be degree, post-graduate or fast-track) and a shorthand speed of 100 words per minute.

How relevant is previous work experience and what sort of placements would you look for?

Andy Cairns: It helps – and people who've been offered places on our own work experience programme have a chance to know how we work, and we have a chance to see their potential.

Suzanne Lord: I am looking for someone who is passionate about news so for me someone who has gone out and got placements or done hospital radio, or worked for their local or community magazine, is key. It is not always easy to get placements at established broadcasters like the BBC or STV as demand is high, but someone who has gone out and done something is always better.

Lorraine Herbison: Work experience is vital. I would be very doubtful about someone if they had been through school and university and not had much work experience. Work experience changed my own life and it can do that for anyone. I prefer interviewees to have had some form of radio work experience and if they have not asked for any work experience with Bauer while at university, I always ask why. If they have been working elsewhere then it is understandable. Otherwise it is not.

Please list some of the key skills new recruits should have.

Lorraine Herbison: Attitude is so important to me. That and a great work ethic. The desire to do the job combined with a great voice and some basic multimedia journalism skills are key. Ability to use editing equipment for both audio and video and writing tight, short scripts for commercial radio are also key skills. Shorthand is useful but not vital.

Suzanne Lord: Listening is a great skill, as is being inquisitive and a thirst to find out more. In terms of technical-based skills, all of that can be taught. For me it comes down to passion for the job as a journalist and a can-do attitude. It is more than a job.

Andy Cairns: Sports reporting is much more than match reporting, so we prefer candidates with an NCTJ qualification – we know they will have grounding in key areas such as media law, public affairs and news reporting.

How important is good use of English and how do you ascertain this?

Lorraine Herbison: It shocks me how poor students' grammar is. I feel we're fighting a losing battle with this as more and more potential employees have bad grammar and fail to understand its importance. Bad grammar can entirely change a sentence's meaning, so if it is not correct, how can the news reader convey the correct meaning of the story?

Andy Cairns: Precision is key. We look for accuracy in story-telling and people who are clear, concise and precise with their language and use of words. Clarity is more important than over-elaborate sentences.

Suzanne Lord: In an on-screen role or reporting role on digital then good use of English is essential. We would assess this through an interview or screen test or a written practical exercise.

Is a candidate's voice judged?

Lorraine Herbison: A good voice is obviously very important in broadcasting. We had one student in on work experience who made it on air with the top story on his very first day because his voice was so good. Sounding authoritative and confident with a good pace and good diction are the basics. You can develop your personality on air with practice.

Suzanne Lord: Yes, to a certain extent. For an on-screen role having a clear voice is important. However, it is not the clincher. We work with voice coaches to bring out the best natural elements of the voice.

Andy Cairns: Only if applying for an on-air broadcast role. Speech impediments are not a barrier to other roles in broadcasting.

How important is good diction?

Suzanne Lord: Good diction is important.

Lorraine Herbison: This is vital. Regional accents are welcome so long as you pronounce your t's and d's. Some have to work at this harder than others.

Andy Cairns: It's vital for on-air. We encourage a variety of accents – but people must enunciate clearly so viewers and listeners can easily understand.

Do you ask for a minimum shorthand speed?

Suzanne Lord: No, although many people who apply do have shorthand. I was never taught shorthand and it has never held me back.

Lorraine Herbison: No – it is a useful skill to have when covering stories like court cases but not vital.

Andy Cairns: For our work experience and graduate programme we ask for 100 words per minute. We also sponsor a prize for the best NCTJ shorthand student each year – we're fastest with the news and want to encourage the fastest shorthand. It's a vital skill if you're on the phone and want to get news to screen quickly.

Which personal qualities will help an applicant succeed?

Suzanne Lord: I want to see passion for what we do. A can-do attitude is the most important, and someone who does not give up. A lot of what we do is trying to find and set up what initially seems impossible. I want someone who will keep trying and even when it doesn't come off on day one can come back in on day two and on a different story and do the same again with as much energy and enthusiasm.

Lorraine Herbison: An outgoing personality with a positive attitude and a desire to work hard are most important. Someone who is warm and friendly will always find it easier to get interviewees to open up to them.

Andy Cairns: Resilience, determination, curiosity, ability to listen. We look for good attitudes as well – people prepared to work hard over long hours. Television also demands team players.

When advertising posts, do you ask candidates to submit a CV and covering letter or complete an application form?

Suzanne Lord: At STV we usually just ask for a CV and a covering letter.

Andy Cairns: Jobs are advertised on our website, www.workforsky.com, and candidates complete an online application form.

Lorraine Herbison: At Bauer I always ask for a covering letter, CV and demo. CVs should have your work experience up top and your school qualifications at the bottom – not the other way round.

Can you provide any examples of applicants who stood out during the sifting process for good and bad reasons?

Andy Cairns: Avoid spelling mistakes and poor grammar. Badly written accompanying letters, writing about yourself in the third person, and sending in vague and generic applications are virtually guaranteed to receive a rejection letter. The best applications are tailored to the employer and demonstrate why the applicant wants to work there.

Suzanne Lord: Candidates who have stood out have put in lots of preparation. They know the product and they have an opinion on it. They may also have put in the effort to try to find out about what we want by speaking to people in the company. I never mind speaking to a candidate before an interview, even if I am on the panel. The big thing for me is ideas.

Lorraine Herbison: I get so annoyed when someone addresses a job application to Sir/Madam when applicants have been asked to specifically email me. I also bin applications without a demo. I am also often tempted to bin work experience applications addressed to Sir/Madam. They are not going to go very far in journalism if they cannot be bothered to find out who is in charge of the newsroom.

If you require a demo what should it comprise?

Suzanne Lord: We will only ask for demos for on-screen roles like reporters and presenters. It should be short (two or three minutes) and show a selection of work. It should always have a piece to camera in it or a live if you have one.

Andy Cairns: Only for on-air roles. Short, sharp with relevant clips. If applying for a sports reporter role then don't include clips involving showbiz interviews! And you'd be amazed how many people applying for reporter positions include stories all about themselves skydiving, water-skiing or driving a rally car. We're not interested!

Lorraine Herbison: If you are applying for a bulletin editor role where the main job is news reading then a demo should ideally be similar to a Bauer news bulletin. If you are applying for a reporter role you should demonstrate the range of stories you have worked on. However, the main thing I am looking out for is the voice, so any example where you are broadcasting would give me an idea of how you sound.

What form does an interview with your company take?

Suzanne Lord: It is usually a panel interview with two or three people from the relevant teams. Sometimes we ask HR to sit on the panel. We ask a range of questions designed to bring out the skills and experience relevant to the job. There are often scenario-based questions which we use to test legal and editorial knowledge. Sometimes, we do a practical test. This might be a screen test for a presenter or a written test for a production journalist.

Lorraine Herbison: There are usually two people interviewing the applicant – myself and one of the news editors. We begin with a chat with the interviewee. This is followed by various core competency tests such as a running order test, legal and style test, feature ideas test, a voicer, a scenario and a voice test. After these we have another chat and that is the candidate's chance to ask us questions.

Andy Cairns: Graduate and apprentice schemes start with an assessment day with around 10-12 candidates. Even if this doesn't lead to a job it offers great learning experience and can lead to an opening at a later date and help prepare you for other job interviews. Other job interviews here will be with a formal panel – usually including at least two senior journalists.

How would you advise an applicant to prepare for an interview?

Suzanne Lord: Watch the programmes, look at the website and have an opinion about what we do. I will always ask what we can do better. I am less interested in what we do well. Critique the programme – it makes me think you have taken a real interest in it. Also speak to people who work in the newsroom. You should always be given the names of the people on the panel. I never mind speaking to people beforehand to chat about what I want from the ideal candidate. Other interviewers may say no but you have lost nothing if they do. It all goes to show how keen you are. I would always prepare for the 'Why do you want the job?' question. It is an easy one and to have that in your back pocket helps you get over any nerves.

Andy Cairns: Ask your course to run some practice interviews. Be across the news, especially the way it's being covered by the organisation interviewing you. Make sure you've watched, read, or listened to the news over the previous week. Dress appropriately for the occasion. A digital start-up may not expect a smart look but a traditional newspaper probably would. If in doubt, phone and ask. And have some questions of your own for the interview panel. There's usually an opportunity to ask at the end.

Lorraine Herbison: Listen to our bulletins and find

out how Bauer works. Also get to know the patch as we are all about local news.

What makes a bad interview?

Lorraine Herbison: If you don't prepare, you will fail in the interview. I once interviewed a girl who just crumbled and had no real answer for anything we were asking her. She had no ideas for news stories or features and we brought the interview to a quick end.

Suzanne Lord: I will always ask what story ideas people have. A reply of 'that's a good question' signals to me they don't have any. A candidate who wants the job will come with several ideas and also know how they will translate to the output. It gets my goat when they haven't watched the programme and can't demonstrate they know what we do. Again, lack of ideas is very poor. As journalists we should always be thinking about things which will make a story.

Andy Cairns: Don't bluff! The interview panel will see through it.

Any final tips?

Lorraine Herbison: Be prepared to move location for a job. We have some starter positions at some of our smaller stations. You may have to consider moving away from where you studied to get a foot in the door. Remember, this is never a nine-to-five job. Your phone should be on at all times, and if you don't want a job that may require you to work on evenings and weekends, then this is not the career for you. My work ethic has always been 'work hard, play hard'. This can be a really fun industry to be part of, but believe me you can only 'play hard' if you work hard. Laziness and a bad attitude will always be found out.

Andy Cairns: Make the most of your time on your training course. Grab every opportunity. Gain experience on the course website, TV, radio, and print publications. Demand that your course leaders organise accompanied visits to court, inquests, council meetings, parliament, and company annual general meetings. You need to understand how these work so you hit the ground running when you land a job. Same with sport: demand accompanied visits to sports events so you see how journalists work, what the etiquette is, and how news-gathering works. If you're on an NCTJ course aim for the Gold Standard. It really helps give you the edge in that search for a job. There's a good chance that first job may be a self-employed freelance. So ask your training centre to put on a session explaining how freelancing works – how to set up as a freelance, how to pitch for work, how to invoice and run your business.

Suzanne Lord: Be keen, show interest and make your mark. If you do work shadowing, try to be involved and ask questions. Before you leave make sure you ask if there are any opportunities coming up. Try also to keep in contact with people once you have gone. If you are unsuccessful after an interview then ask for feedback. No one ever minds doing it. You will find out very useful things so that next time you are better prepared. It is also a chance to find out a bit more about what is going on in the place you have applied to – maybe they have more opportunities coming up. It's a conversation that is never wasted!

APPLYING FOR JOBS

Many organisations require candidates to fill out application forms, others ask for a cover letter and CV. If you are asked to submit the latter, above all else, make sure you tailor each letter and CV to the organisation and precise job for which you are applying. There is no such thing as a winning 'stock' CV or cover letter. Employers hate them.

Cover letter

Letters should be no longer than one page of A4 comprising three or four short paragraphs. Use a well-known font like Cambria or Arial and a font size of 10-12. As with all formal letters your address should be top right with the date immediately below. The recipient's details should be top left.

Your writing should be short and to the point. You're introducing yourself to a prospective employer. Sell yourself, without directly repeating detail from your CV. Ensure any claims you make are backed up in the accompanying CV. Do not tell lies or exaggerate. You will be found out.

Always address the letter to the pertinent person. 'Dear Sir or Madam' will not cut it, especially in the media. If you haven't bothered to find out the correct name and title of the head of news at your local commercial radio station, he or she is unlikely to employ you. You have just shown you have no research skills, you are lazy, or both. In the top line refer to the name of the role for which you are applying and state any reference numbers.

The cover letter should make clear you have knowledge of the company, so make sure you do some research. Make a positive reference to something the organisation promotes, sells or values but do not gush. Say why you want the job in terms of your own career and highlight skills, experience and personal qualities you possess which link directly to the job description.

Avoid using employment clichés like 'good team player' and 'capable of working on one's own initiative'. Instead prove you have these qualities through examples in your CV. End your letter on a positive note such as 'I look forward to hearing from you' and sign off with 'Yours sincerely' as you have, remember, addressed the letter to a named person.

On occasion it's worth thinking outside the box and creating a cover letter with a difference. I've seen eye-catching letters designed as press releases, adverts, even news copy, and these can be highly effective in grabbing attention in the right environment.

Make sure there are no errors. Spelling, grammar and punctuation must be perfect. Don't rely on a computerised spelling and grammar check – they often use American English and won't flag up all errors. Go over the letter several times and give it to someone (who has a good grasp of English) to check.

CV (curriculum vitae)

This is where you start to prove you're the right person for the job. It's all about relevance, so as with a news story, you must grab the reader's attention by putting the most relevant information up top.

Your CV should be no more than two sides of A4. Include your name and contact details at the top, potentially in a header, and remember to include links to any blogs or portfolios. There's no need to write CV in huge capital letters – talk about stating the obvious and a waste of space...

Depending on your stage in life it will either start with career history or work experience, with the most recent first. Underline categories such as Work Experience. Use bold for employers' names and, if relevant, your roles. If your career is already underway, start with a Career History clearly stating employers' names, your job titles and dates:

> *Career History*
> *BBC Radio Scotland – Reporter*
> *August 2016 - present.*

Give details of each role you have held, firmly bearing in mind the description of the job for which you are now applying. Mention experience, skills and qualities being sought by your prospective employers. In a CV do not quote 'reasons for leaving' as sometimes asked for on an application form. If you have been promoted within an organisation or won an award, make sure you mention it.

After you have exhausted your employment history and/or work experience, move on to qualifications and education, with the most recent first. Professional qualifications (such as an NCTJ diploma) should be mentioned ahead of educational achievements. Name academic institutions and your dates of study but only include higher, further and secondary education. Keep secondary education information short, stating the name of your school and exam results only. When listing exam results such as Highers, start with the highest grade you achieved (e.g. English – A, French – B and so on). With degrees, only include the honours classification if it is a 2:1 or better.

It's no bad thing to mention non-career related employment such as a part-time bar job while at university. It's always good to show you're able to hold down a job, regardless of what it is.

Students still at university, who are sending a CV in order to secure a work placement, should start with any previous work experience followed by details of their current university or college course. Detail relevant modules studied which will be of interest to the organisation to which you're applying.

Hobbies and Interests?

I'm not convinced prospective employers are terribly interested in your interests, but if you have space to fill by all means mention specific non-controversial hobbies: golf, archery, football etc. Socialising is not a hobby, nor is going to the pub. A pastime which subtly highlights your suitability for the job, such as being a volunteer football coach, would clearly be appropriate when applying for a football-related job. You can also use this section to show you're good at something (e.g. keen golfer – handicap 4). Obviously this would be especially relevant if your extensive pre-application research revealed your prospective new boss to be a fanatical golfer. It can be helpful to title this section Additional Information as you can then include other, more relevant information such as a full, clean driving licence.

At the end you may include the names, job titles and contact details of two referees, at least one of whom should be your current employer or an academic referee. Try to choose referees relevant to your prospective employer – so if you were applying for the position of news assistant at STV and had done work experience in the newsroom last summer, your referee could be the person who mentored you during the placement. It's not essential to include referees on your CV, and if you do, ensure you have their permission.

Personal statements

There's great debate about the merit of including a personal statement, sometimes called a mission statement, in CVs. If you're sending a covering letter, there's generally no need. What you would say in your mission statement has already been conveyed.

A personal or mission statement is usually a summary of up to 150 words which details your general fabulousness. All too often they are filled with run-of-the-mill claims. Everyone is: friendly, hard-working, highly motivated, creative, a team player, a leader, or at the very least, they are ambitious. Personal/mission statements are generally more appropriate for people who are already on the career ladder than those attempting to get on to the first rung.

Photographs

In the UK most employers do not expect you to include a photograph with a job application. Actors are the exception.

Other considerations

It goes without saying your CV must be accurate, in terms of information, spelling, grammar and punctuation. The layout should make it easy to read.

Don't use company logos on your CV. They may add a welcome splash of colour but technically they are protected by intellectual property laws and should not be used without permission.

One last thing...

Most job applications are made online but if you're sending your CV by post use an A4 envelope so you don't have to fold it and it doesn't arrive creased.

HOW WAS IT FOR YOU?

In this final chapter, former journalism students who are now making it in the industry, share their thoughts on what it's like to work in the media. As true journalists, they tell it like it is. Be prepared for some colourful language.

Describe your current job.

Ronnie Charters, sports reporter, Radio Clyde: My role involves going to the press conferences of Scottish clubs and providing content for Radio Clyde and the rest of the Bauer network in Scotland (including Radio Tay, Radio Forth, Northsound, etc.). As well as that I cover football matches including Scotland, European, and domestic games, and provide live reports from them to the show on air. My job is very much a 24/7 job, as the ever-evolving world of social media means we must be switched on constantly to what stories are breaking in order to be ahead of our competitors.

John Callan, broadcast journalist, Bauer Media: I'm a radio bulletin editor, so I spend most of my time writing and editing copy, editing audio, reading bulletins, sourcing stories and putting news online. It's absolutely not what I thought I'd end up doing when I first started studying journalism, but I love it. I cover all sorts of subjects and my day moves at a million miles an hour. You're immediately reacting to things happening and putting them in plain terms for people to understand them with you. I think that's pretty exciting.

Sahil Jaidka, chief sub-editor, Sky Sports News: I lead and support a team of multi-platform journalists, overseeing key editorial decisions, ensuring the teams are producing the best sports news content to digital and linear platforms and being responsible for the content and direction of output. I regularly spend time in the gallery, producing output for Sky Sports News, Sky News sports bulletins, skysports.com and third-party clients. This involves deciding on running orders and story treatments. Furthermore, I live produce on location, with Wimbledon being an example, and decide on how the organisation covers events. I also oversee our breaking news SMS/MMS messages, push notifications on the app and our content on social media.

Liam Bruce, broadcast journalist, That's Thames Valley: I am a broadcast journalist producing daily TV news packages in the Thames Valley area. As well as this I am standby presenter, and duty editor of the station. In cases where the station manager is not present, I am in charge of station content.

Amy Dunsmuir, news organiser, STV: I'm currently working as a news organiser with STV News in Glasgow. I do a whole host of things from setting up stories and getting the latest lines to ongoing stories, to organising where reporters and camera crews need to be. On a 'normal' day I'll be the first point of call for all reporters who are out in story – they'll phone me to let me know how they're getting on and what they'll be able to provide for the programme. I then need to relay this to the producer so they know what to expect. I'll help gather material in from other news centres across Scotland and the UK, speak to other media outlets around the world and will talk to people who get in touch with stories. It's a busy but really rewarding job – at the end of the day I can sit back and watch knowing that none of it would have happened without me. Big-headed, maybe, but I'm the master of the spinning plates to make sure everything (hopefully) comes together.

Calum Leslie, sports journalist, Sky News Radio: The sports team at Sky News Radio provides material to radio stations 24/7. It's relentless some days. It can feel a bit like air-traffic control when you're glued to a chair for nine hours at a time. But I've been lucky enough to cover FA Cup finals, Euro 2016 and Wimbledon – and even grabbed a word (almost literally a single word) with Usain Bolt.

What's the atmosphere like in a professional broadcast newsroom?

John Callan: There are a few things I've found to be true wherever I've worked. Wherever I've been, newly trained journalists are always given a decent amount of trust and responsibility very quickly. Within hours of being in a newsroom, you could be out on a big story with famous journalists you've watched on telly or rolled your eyes at on Twitter.

Ronnie Charters: Having just started my professional career in journalism and having experienced my first professional newsroom, the one thing that has surprised me is the harmonious communal spirit of the journalists. Coming in as the youngest person in the team by quite a few years, I was rather nervous living up to the reputation of the company. However, I cannot put into words the helpful and kind-natured atmosphere in the newsroom. Yes, it is fast-moving and competitive in terms of pushing each other to strive and be the best, and I do feel there is a pressure to continually produce the best quality news output, but the togetherness and comradely nature of the team makes it a productive and successful newsroom.

Sahil Jaidka: No two days are ever the same, so going into the office doesn't always feel like work because of the vibe and passion about the place (also because I'm working within sport so I can't complain!). Now don't get me wrong, we all have our tough days, but one thing I would say is there is a great team spirit within the organisation where people (from all departments) pull together to get everyone through it and get the job done to the standards we set of ourselves. Yes, it's competitive, we all want to excel in our jobs, get that next promotion and really push ourselves, but it's a healthy competitiveness which actually encourages people to do better at their jobs and the result of that is better output. So the atmosphere in short: fun – yes; energetic – yes; on certain nights, crazy – yes; fast paced – yes; competitive – yes; tolerant – yes; stressful – yes; somewhere you want to be – yes.

Colin Stone, senior reporter, Radio Clyde: It's a fast-moving place to be, and the tolerance for mistakes is low. You might get a free pass now and then, but you're expected to be on top of your game every day.

In bigger newsrooms, there's definitely more unspoken competition too: through the work you do, you're trying to show producers and senior staff members that you're better than your colleagues and are capable of handling bigger stories. The camaraderie and friendships you have with your competitors have surprised me. Some of my good friends work for our rival radio station, and when working at STV, I used to speak to several of my colleagues at the BBC. That may sound strange, yes – but when you see these people almost every day at press calls or media events, you get to know each other quite well.

What are the main pressures?

John Callan: Time – I feel like it's a constant game of prioritising. Sometimes I get that wrong, but you have to get good at working out what's a big deal and what isn't. There are some things which aren't worth going to the stake over and some things which are. Obviously, it's pretty public too. So any mistakes you make could get picked up on by anyone. But I feel you do get used to that the more you go on. I also have plenty of work anxiety dreams. Normally, I'm about to read the news live and all my scripts disappear, or none of my audio will fire, or I'm locked out of the studio. I struggle without a script – but I know some colleagues who can very aptly dance around that kind of thing without letting the listeners know anything is wrong. They are geniuses.

Sahil Jaidka: Mainly the ones you put on yourself. We all want to be the best, produce the best content across all our platforms and really give the viewers what they want. We want to be first, we need to always be accurate, we want to be engaging, we need to be adaptable to viewers' wants (social, digital and linear). I think in this industry now it's all about making sure we've served the viewer with all the best stories, but not just on TV. The pressure to get this consistent on digital, on the app, on social media and on TV is huge, but one you thrive off.

Colin Stone: There is not enough time in the day. I'd love to be able to give every package the time it deserves but a lesson I learned very quickly is not to be precious over my content. Most of the time, the work is routine. 10:00 get to work, 10:30 go to shoot, 12:30 back to office to begin edit, 14:30 write rest of programme, 16:30 begin pre-record, 18:00 get show out and go home. *Then repeat.* Such days are fast and the actual story often passes one by. Being first is probably the main pressure. You have the stories which every news outlet gets – photo calls, ministerial visits, government announcements – but when it comes to the breaking stories (mass casualty events, usually), the pressure is on to have the facts before anyone else and to be the first to publish them.

What happens when a journalist makes a mistake?

Claire McAllister, broadcast journalist, BBC Scotland: In the past three years of working in journalism I can only think of being given one real bollocking. In my previous job I once deleted a TV bulletin running order while on air. It all just disappeared. The scripts, pictures, packages – the lot. I had been trying to work ahead to my next bulletin and edited in the wrong one. We managed to restore it without anyone at home noticing but the director came out angry. But to be honest I thought it was a fair way to deal with it. Also, everyone has their bugbears. An anchorman at the TV station I used to work in is pedantic about clichés. Once, when he overheard me recording a football match report, he came over to intervene when he heard me say 'blah, blah, found the back of the net'. He told me not to state the obvious by explicitly saying things that people were watching – pretty spot on advice when you work in telly.

John Callan: Your boss is never likely to be thrilled by a mistake. I don't think I've ever had the hairdryer treatment, but there've been a few phone slams and choice words. If you know you've made one, I always feel it's better to 'fess up straight away.

Amy Dunsmuir: If there's an issue with something that you've written then they'll come and speak to you, tell you why it was wrong and how you could have fixed it. The one thing to remember is, if you're ever unsure about something you're writing, get it checked. I've been working in news for years now and will still ask someone more senior than me to check my copy when I'm writing about a court case.

Calum Leslie: From a local radio news desk to UK-wide broadcasters, incorrect facts cause the most problems. They shouldn't happen, but we're all human. So it's just as important to know what to do after a mistake. Once the "oh f*ck!" moment's passed: forget your pride, own up and make it right as quickly as possible. Bosses will never be delighted – but they will want you to be honest and clear about it.

Describe the upsides and downsides of working in broadcast news.

Claire McAllister: Anti-social working hours are a downside. A lot of work goes into things that only last between 20 seconds and three minutes. When you get it wrong, you really feel the failure in your gut and unfortunately everyone else will get to see that you got it wrong.

John Callan: It's very enjoyable. You get to do fun things you never could in a 'proper' job (as my granny would call anything that isn't a career in the civil service) and I feel there's a lot of variation day-to-day. I don't think there's anything quite like the buzz of nailing an exclusive story.

Roxy McCrae, video-journalist, That's Cumbria: One of the upsides to TV is the buzz you get from covering a big story, or even just a good one. Reporting in TV means you get to build each story from start to finish, visually. So, when covering anything at all, you must always be thinking about what pictures will fit and what road you should take the viewer down, as they learn about the story. This is where the creative side of journalism can flourish and I love every second of it.

Colin Stone: I love the immediacy of news. We're constantly working towards the next hour, the next bulletin; if something happens at 11.30am, our listeners know about it by midday. I also enjoy the satisfaction of getting a story that you've worked really hard on to air.

Amy Dunsmuir: This is where I get all soppy and will probably make some people (myself included) feel a bit sick. It's a cliché but one of the best things about the job is being at the heart of big events. During my short career I've helped cover some of the biggest stories in Scotland over the last few decades. I've covered the horrible incident of the George Square bin lorry accident, the independence referendum and Brexit, to name a few. I've seen major politicians come and go and I've been one of the people responsible for telling the world about it. I've also had the opportunity to meet some utterly amazing people, and I don't just mean celebrities. Being a journalist gives you the chance to see people at their worst, but also at their absolute best, and it's a privilege to be able to tell their stories. It can be really stressful and the hours can be long. It can mean having to stand outside in the snow for hours on end without eating or going to the toilet. It can mean having to knock on the doors of people who have recently lost a loved one. It's definitely not a bed of roses. But, if you truly love it and know that it's the place you belong, those things really don't seem so bad.

Ronnie Charters: I get to do what I have dreamed about my entire life. Firstly, to work on radio, but to report on Scottish football, be involved in some of the most talked about stories and sporting events of the year and interview some of the greatest people on the planet. I get to go to some of the most high-profile sporting occasions and get paid to do so – I really cannot complain.

Calum Leslie: Downsides: you can earn more money in another industry, you can work better hours in another industry, you can be less stressed and drink less coffee and sleep more in another industry. But if you want to do the job at this stage, you'll probably know that already.

What do you wish you'd known, done, or done differently before you entered the profession?

Ronnie Charters: If I were to do anything differently, I would have been more stringent in my diction and voice coaching from the outset. I can admit I neglected my voice training until I really began to see a career in radio, at which point I focused a lot of attention on my voice. I would encourage any budding journalist looking to get into broadcasting to work on your voice and diction at every possible moment. Towards the end of my university career I found myself practising in the car, in my bedroom, in the shower – anytime I had a chance. I only wish I would have done it earlier to train my voice even more.

Amy Dunsmuir: It's not really something I wish I'd known, more something I wish I'd done sooner – not taking things personally. It can be disheartening when a story you've set up doesn't make it on to the programme and it can be really upsetting when you get a phone call from a viewer who's shouting at you for something. At first I used to take this sort of stuff to heart and worry about it for ages. It's hard not to. Now though, with a better understanding of how news works, I know not to.

Sahil Jaidka: I wish I'd stuck in at voice coaching at university. I don't want to be a presenter, and you might ask 'why does someone who produces across platforms want a better voice?' Well, it's because you can't ever pigeonhole yourself! You can be out on location producing away, then out of nowhere someone turns up and you could get them live on air and there's no presenter, for example. That's where you can be extra valuable and step in.

Roxy McCrae: I would have benefited from a better education in English language, from an earlier age. It was never my strong point and grammatical errors are my downfall. If I could go back and do anything differently at university it would be to focus on getting that area of my English up to scratch. It is an important part of journalism, no matter the medium, but particularly in broadcast, as everything you write must be in present tense and follow that rule throughout.

What advice would you give someone starting out in the industry?

Claire McAllister: Always be able to justify your choices – that's some of the earliest and best advice I was given. After my first week producing the morning bulletins I remember my line manager asking me why I put a certain story above another. I felt sick, told him why and he just nodded and walked away. So I panicked assuming I'd messed up. It took me until the next afternoon to ask him about it. To begin with, he barely remembered the conversation, and then he repeated that very advice. I hadn't messed up. I was relieved, and the reminder about justifying choices has stayed with me.

Colin Stone: Don't expect lunch breaks.

Calum Leslie: There isn't a manual for *everything* you'll face in this job. Knowing your stuff's clearly important. But news is just that – new – and a lot of it involves reacting to events and improvising. It's okay to think 'I've no idea how to tackle this' – and no-one's going to think less of you for asking for advice. The more experience someone's got, the more likely it is they've dealt with something similar. I still do it all the time. So ask, and remember what they say. The one thing that *will* piss people off is repeatedly asking how to do the same thing.

And finally...

Claire McAllister: It was silly o'clock in the morning. I went to present the morning bulletin and saw 'Borussia Mönchengladbach' in the script – the name of a football team. It was the first time I'd come across it. You come across words you don't know how to pronounce all the time – hello Google. I tried to listen to a post-match interview but it was in German which I don't speak. The clock was ticking. I went into the studio thinking I've got to give this a bash. I did not exactly nail it – but I did say it with confidence. I came back in vision to say 'Here's today's weather' with the most apologetic look on my face. Oh it was painful. Fair to say I can say it in my sleep now.

John Callan: On my first day freelancing at one newsroom, I was sent out to staff a political photo-call. I signed out one of the pool cars. Now, I'd been driving for a good seven years by this stage, but never once come across a car with a wee clip on the gearstick, which you need to pull up to put it into reverse. I spent a good 10 minutes frantically flailing around the driver's seat in a bid to back this thing out of its parking space. Eventually, I had to admit defeat and go back inside with my tail between my legs and – in front of all my new colleagues – ask my editor to reverse the car out of the space for me. I never thought I'd work, or be allowed to talk to humans, again.

Sahil Jaidka: After a 16-hour day covering Wimbledon, I finally found time for some dinner before the final press conference. I ran to get a pizza, came back and sat outside the press conference room. Milos Raonic (the man I was waiting for because he was playing Andy Murray in the final) walked out. We said hello and I was just about to open the box and dig in when he sniffed and asked 'is that pizza?' I said it was. Five seconds later, he took the biggest chunk out of my pizza and started munching! I was starving! The best bit was when one of his team ran behind us and said 'I don't think that's gluten free', and his response was 'F*ck off I'm hungry!' Thankfully it didn't help him win, and Andy Murray triumphed. A year later I interviewed Raonic and reminded him of the pizza incident, to which he replied: 'Sometimes in life you gotta do what you gotta do.'

BIBLIOGRAPHY

Boyd, A., 2001. *Broadcast journalism: techniques of radio and television news*. Taylor & Francis.

Casella, P.A., 2013. Breaking News or Broken News?, Journalism Practice, vol. 7, no. 3, pp. 362-376.

Gowers, E., 1986. The complete plain words, revised by Sidney Greenbaum and Janet Whitcut.

Graham, S. and Frank, G., 1958. *Beloved Infidel: the education of a woman*. Holt.

King, S., 2000. On Writing: A Memoir of the Craft. *New York: Scribner.*

Leech, G. and Deuchar, M., R. Hoogenraad (2006). *English grammar for today: a new introduction.*

Orwell, G., 1945. Politics and the English language. *New York, 68.*

Orwell, G., 2014. *Why I write*. Penguin UK.

Strunk Jr, W., 1979. White EB. The elements of style.

Truss, L., 2004. *Eats, shoots & leaves: The zero tolerance approach to punctuation*. Penguin.

White, T. 2005, *Broadcast news: writing, reporting, and producing*. Taylor & Francis.

WEB SOURCES

BBC Breakfast presenter is sent £20 by viewer 'to
fix her northern accent'. Mail Online.
http://www.dailymail.co.uk/news/article-
2847652/BBC-Breakfast-presenter-sent-20-
viewer-fix-northern-accent.html (accessed 27
July 2017)

BBC News style guide. BBC.
www.bbc.co.uk/academy/journalism/news-
style-guide

Farewell Keith Waterhouse: King of Fleet Street
and Daily Mail columnist dies aged 80. With
a special tribute by his friend, Richard
Littlejohn. Mail Online.
http://www.dailymail.co.uk/news/article-
1211242/Keith-Waterhouse-dies-aged-
80.html (accessed June 2017)

28618788R00079

Printed in Great Britain
by Amazon